UNDERPERFORMING BILLBOARD DREAMS

IN NEW ORLEANS

by

Chris Sullivan

All billboards in New Orleans in the fall of 2005 were underperforming; if not rendered absurd or irrelevant by catastrophe, erased by the hurricane to blither like old TV screens tuned to noise. Many would stay that way for months and years where advertisers had no interest targeting a depopulated city beset with basic concerns.

Close to the ground, language sprouted.
Ugly mass produced plastic signs advertising recovery services proliferated. Many took matters into their own hands: for a can of spray paint, shard of plywood and a useful service to proclaim, a person was in business. This book promotes those efforts and imagines the billboard as civic witness, memorial, reflection and marquee for stories from an extraordinary time.

Chris Sullivan
New Orleans, 2007

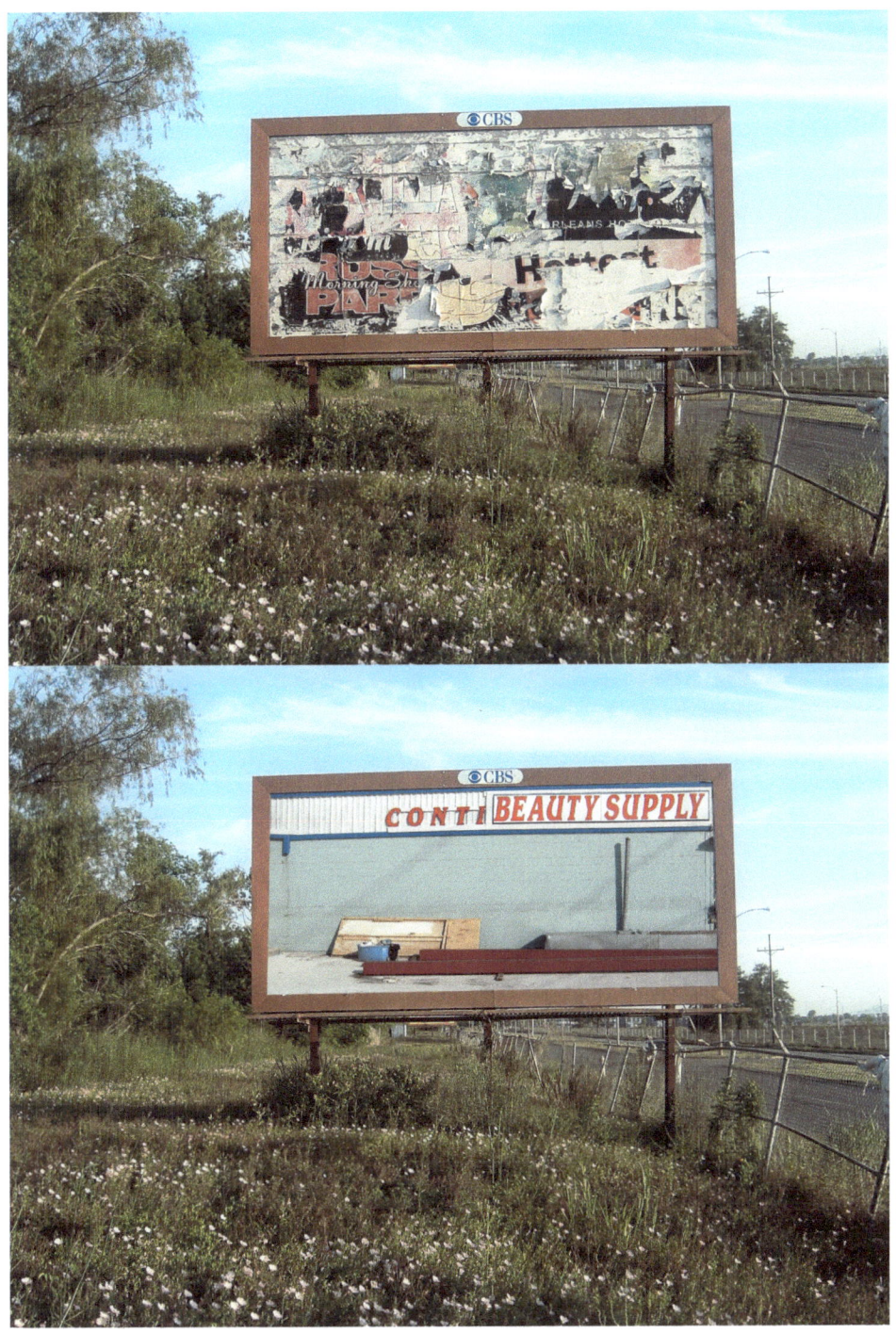

RATLIFF's
USED
CARS
1542 DESIRE ST.
N.O. LA.
948 - 6992

Slight
PUBLICATIONS
thingnamer at gmail
© 2012 ISBN **978-0615973845**

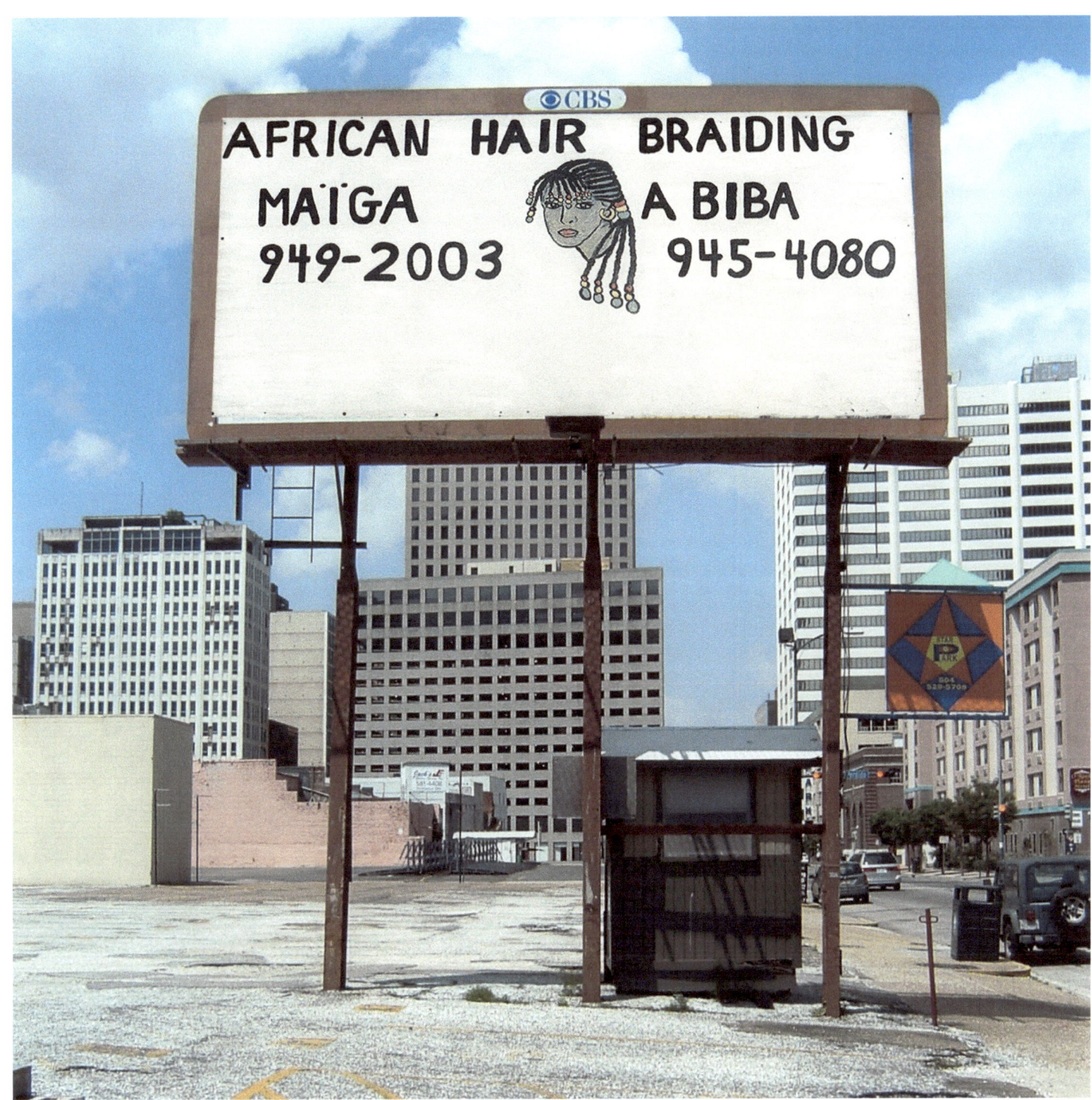

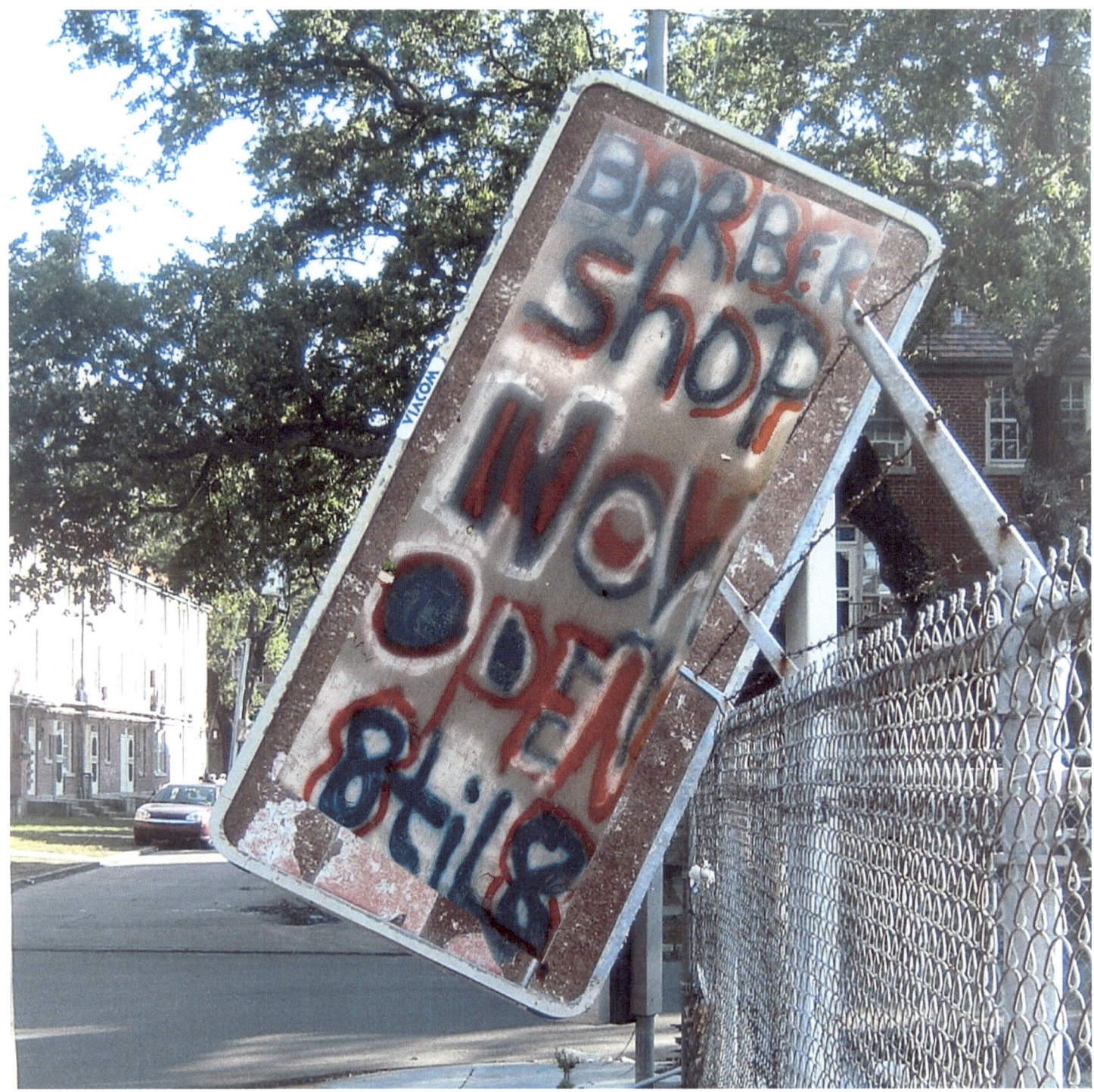

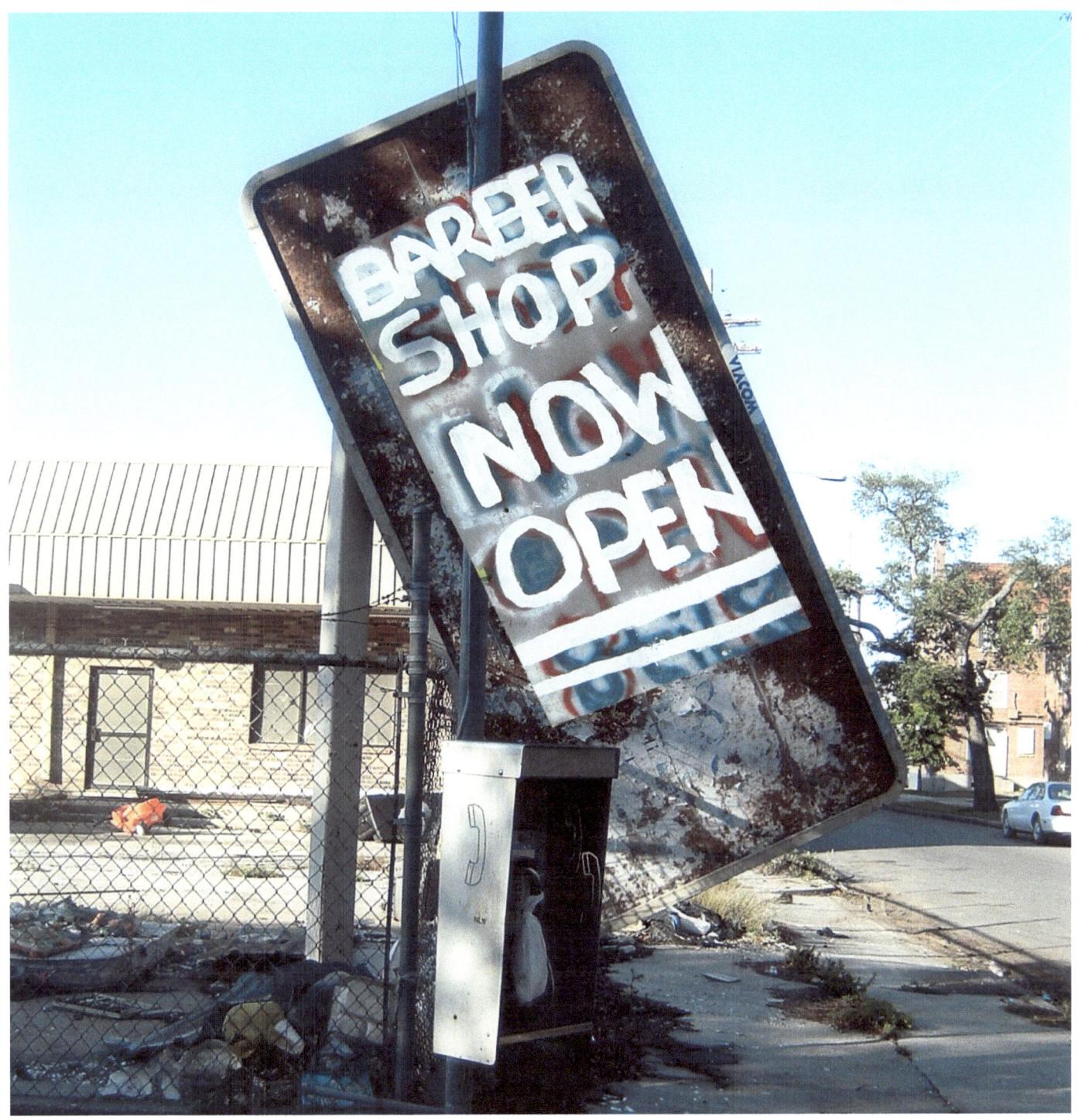

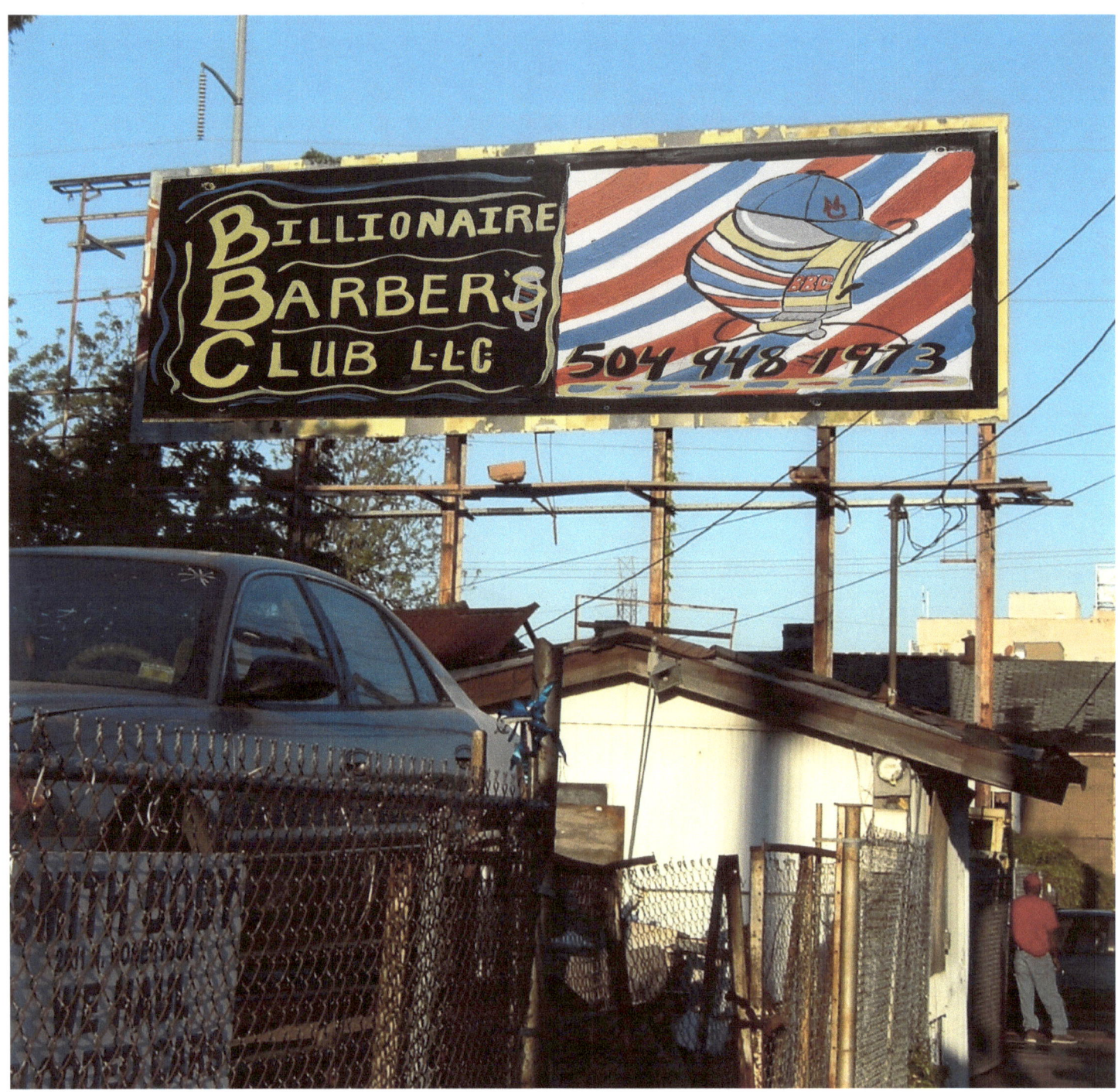

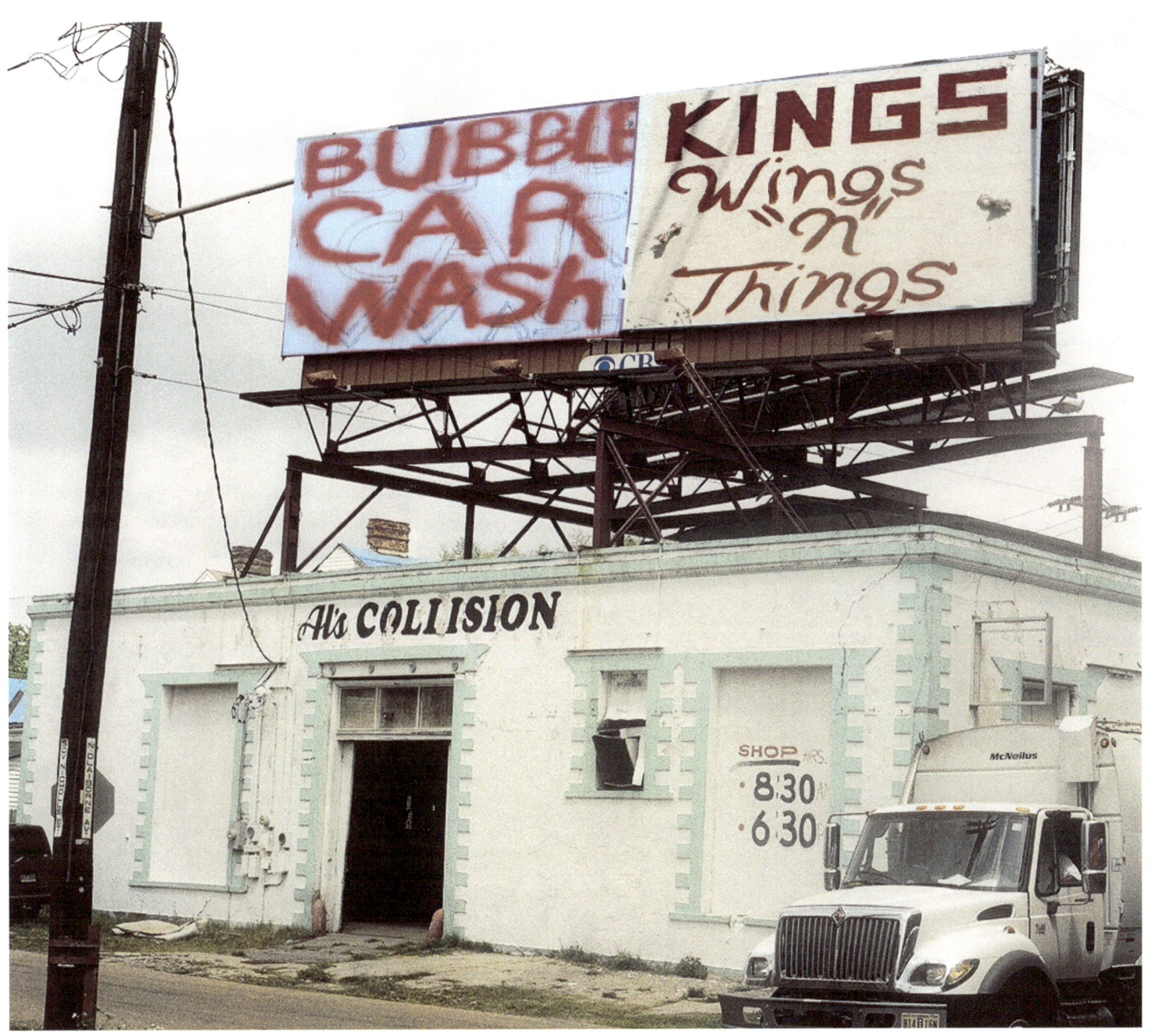

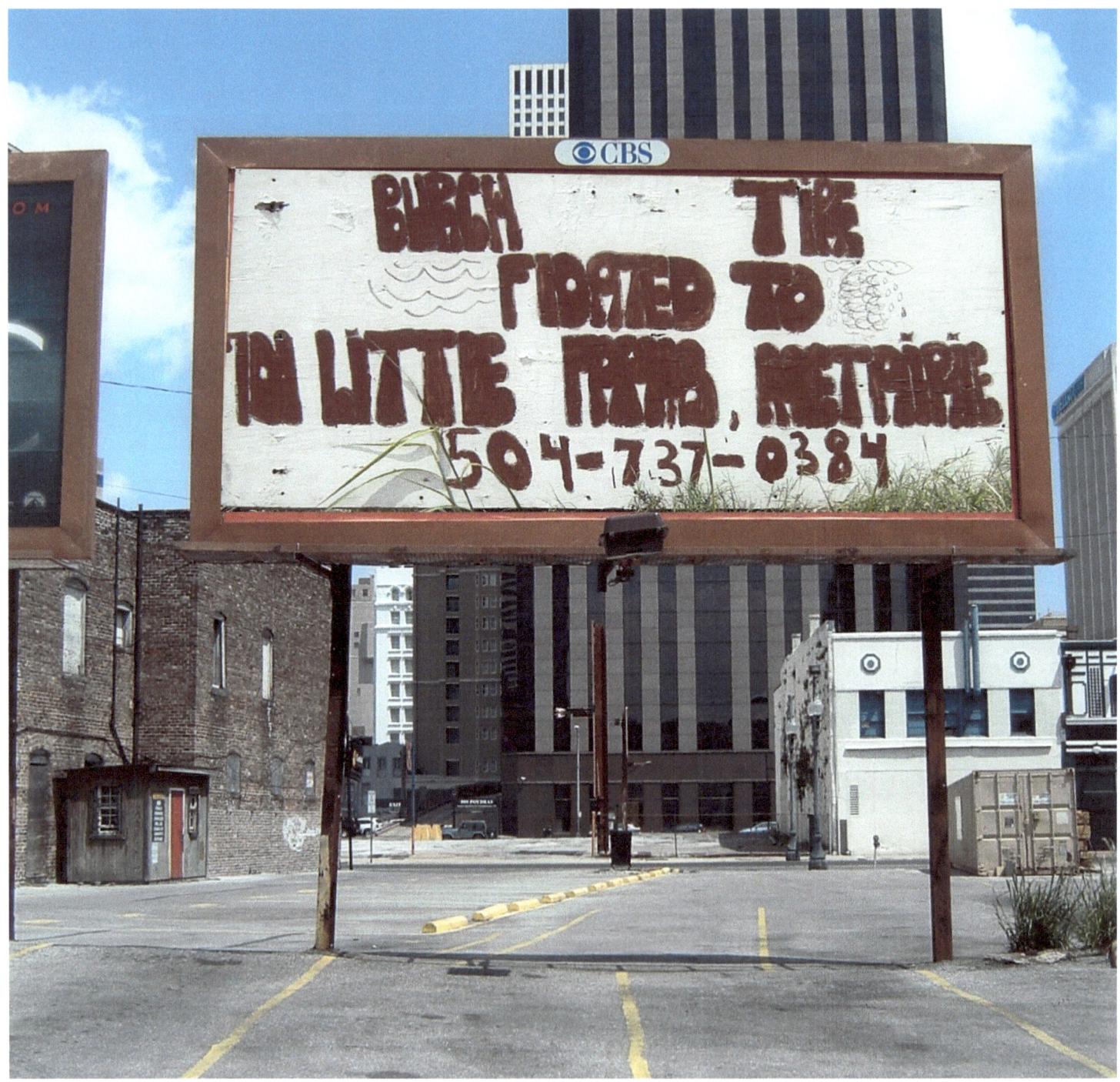

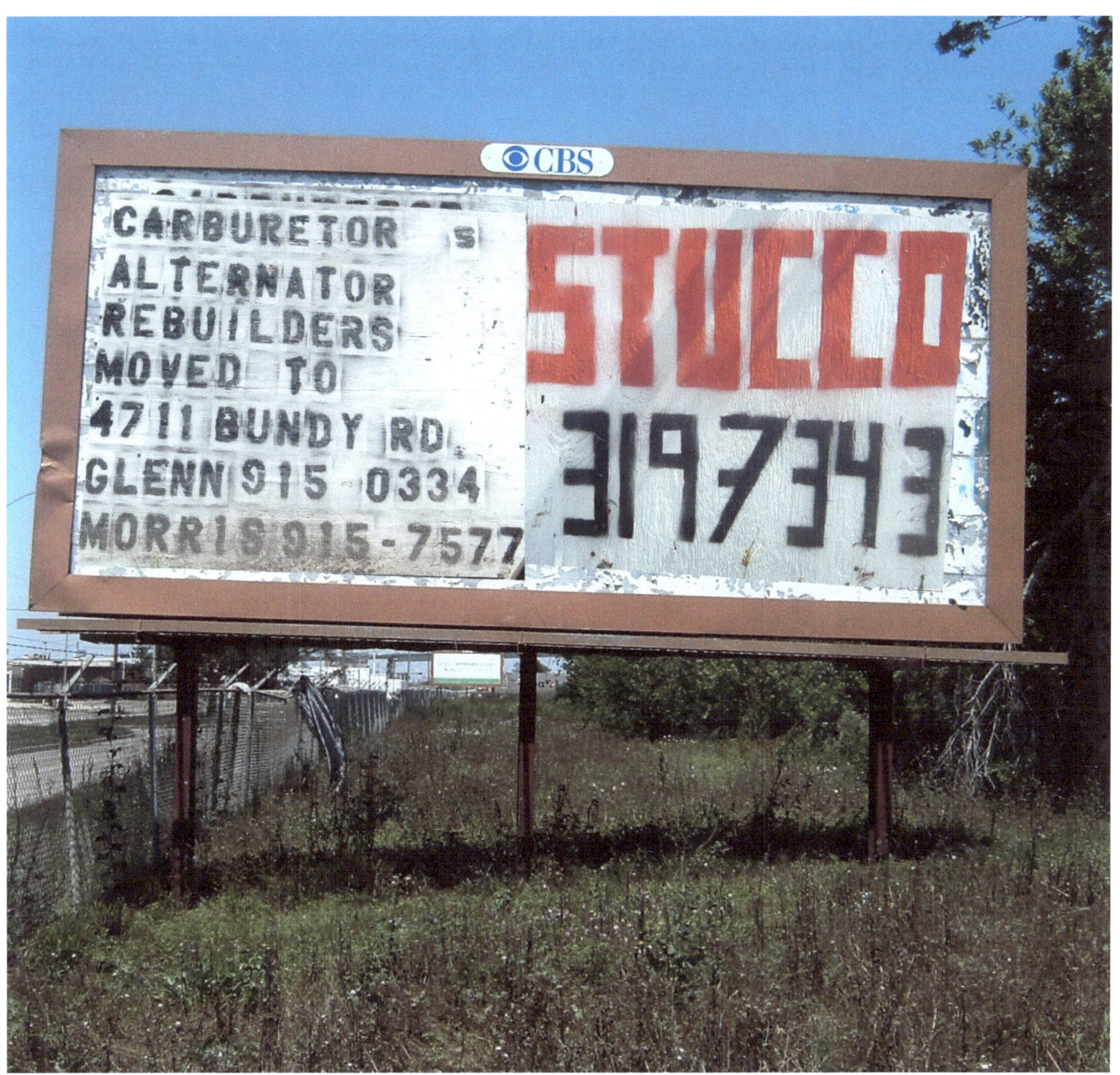

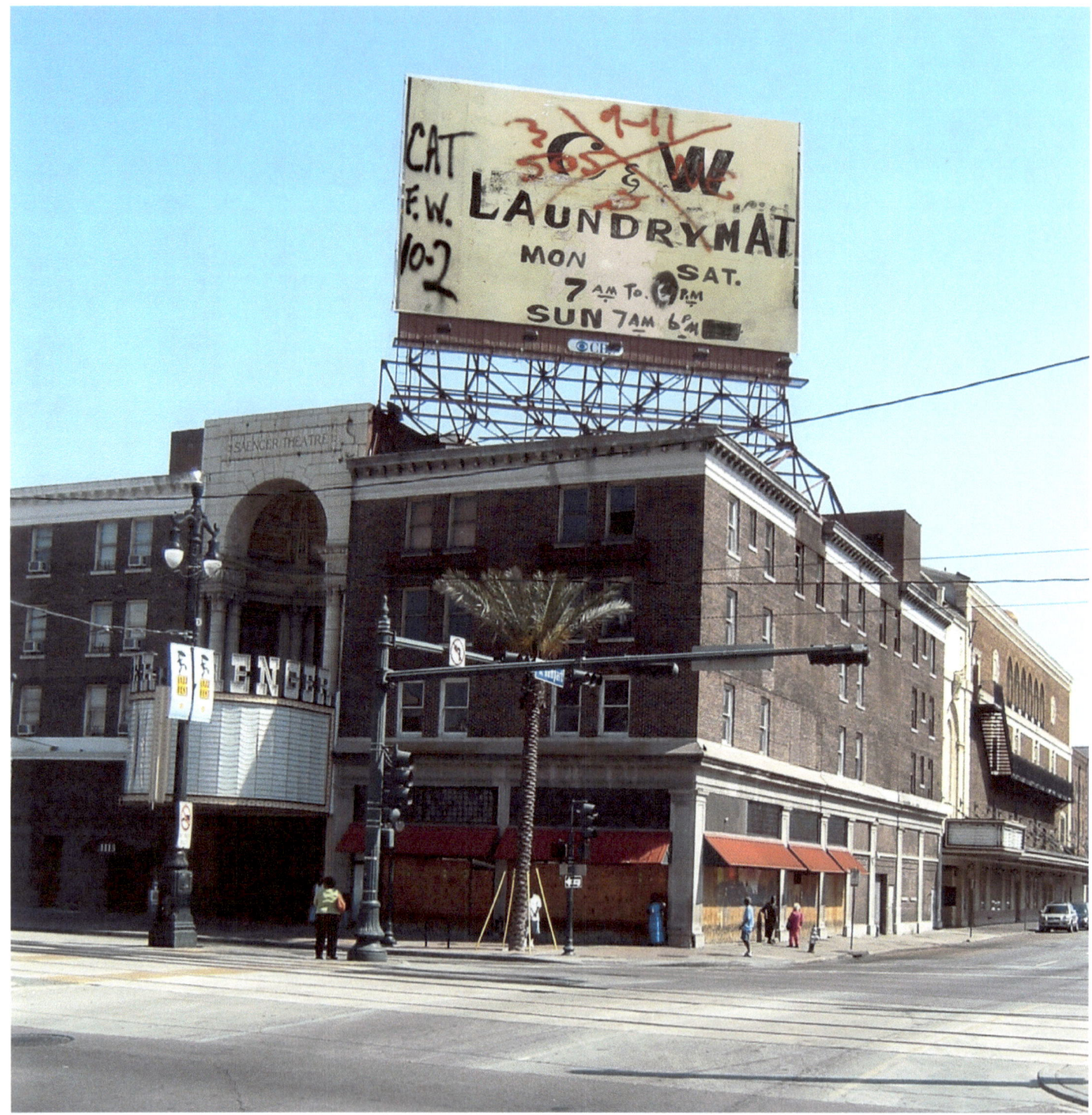

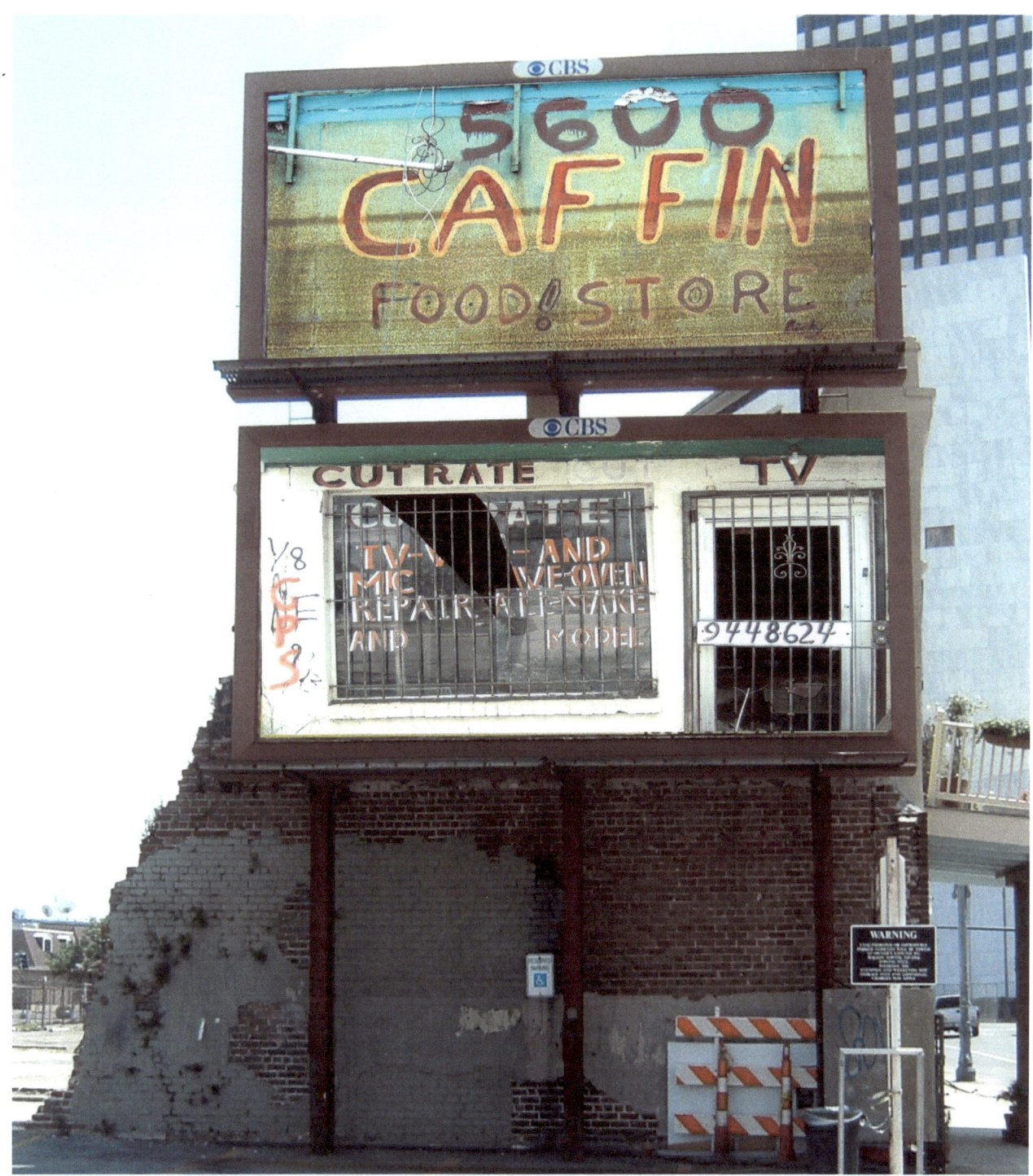

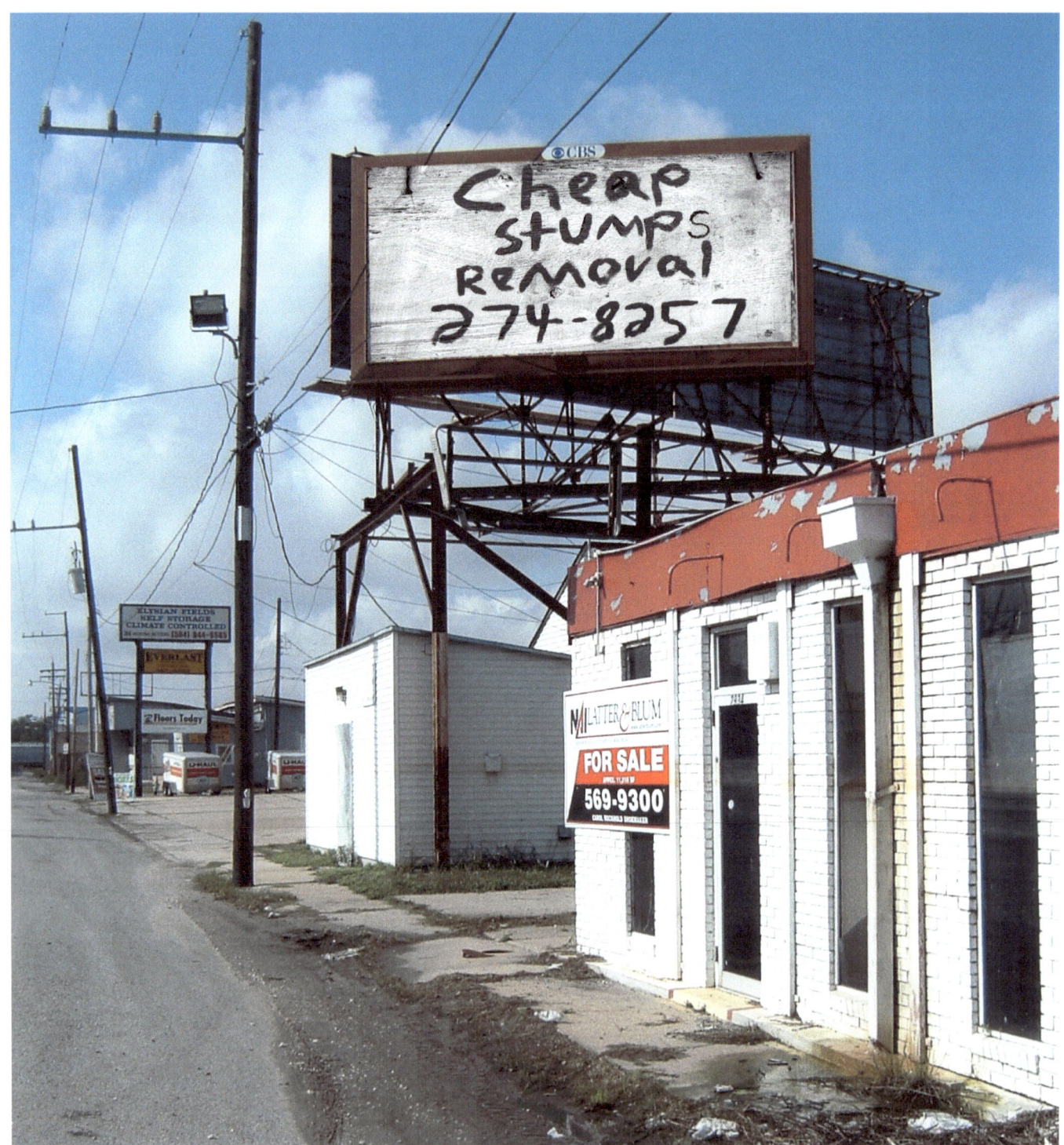

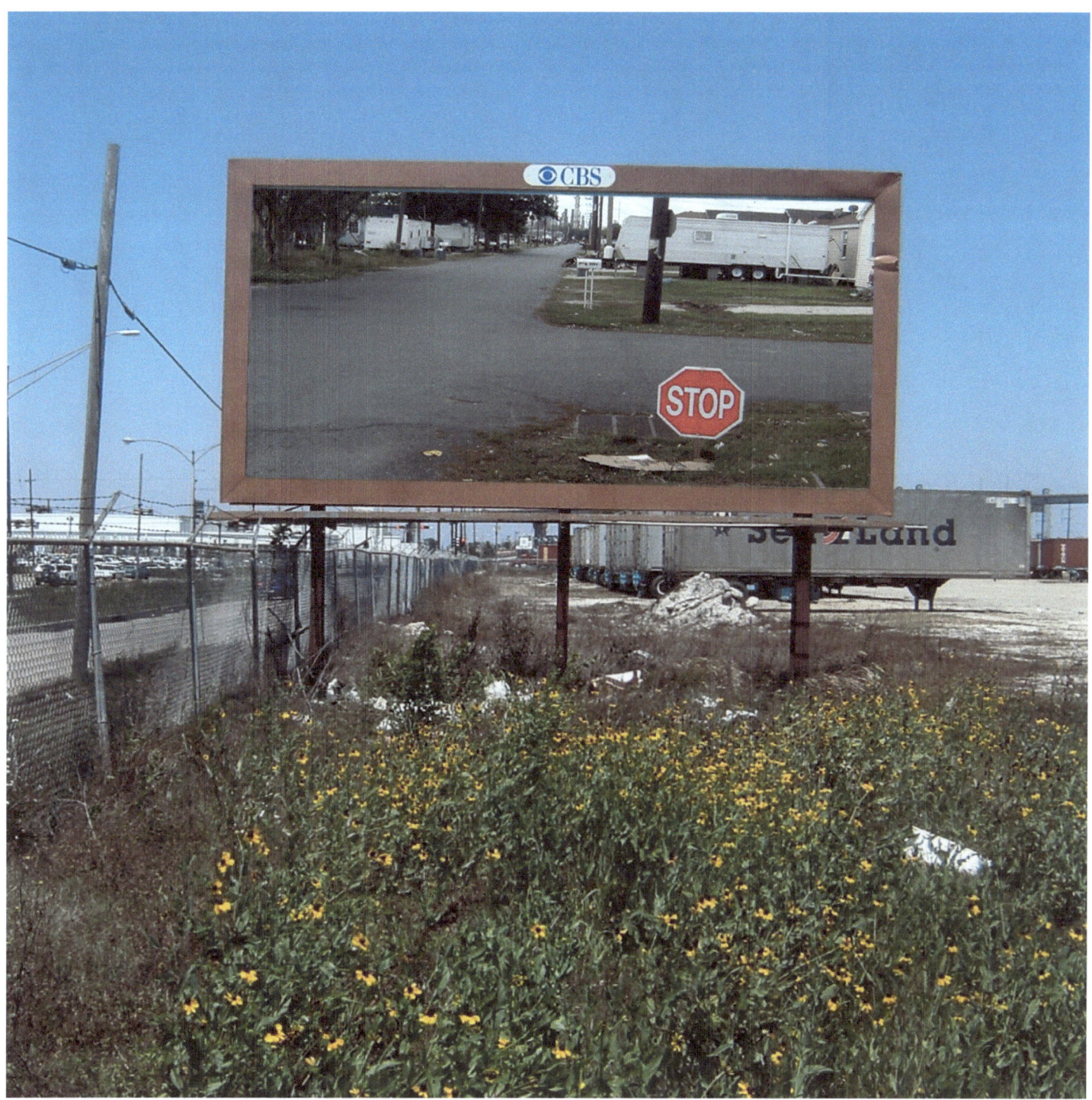

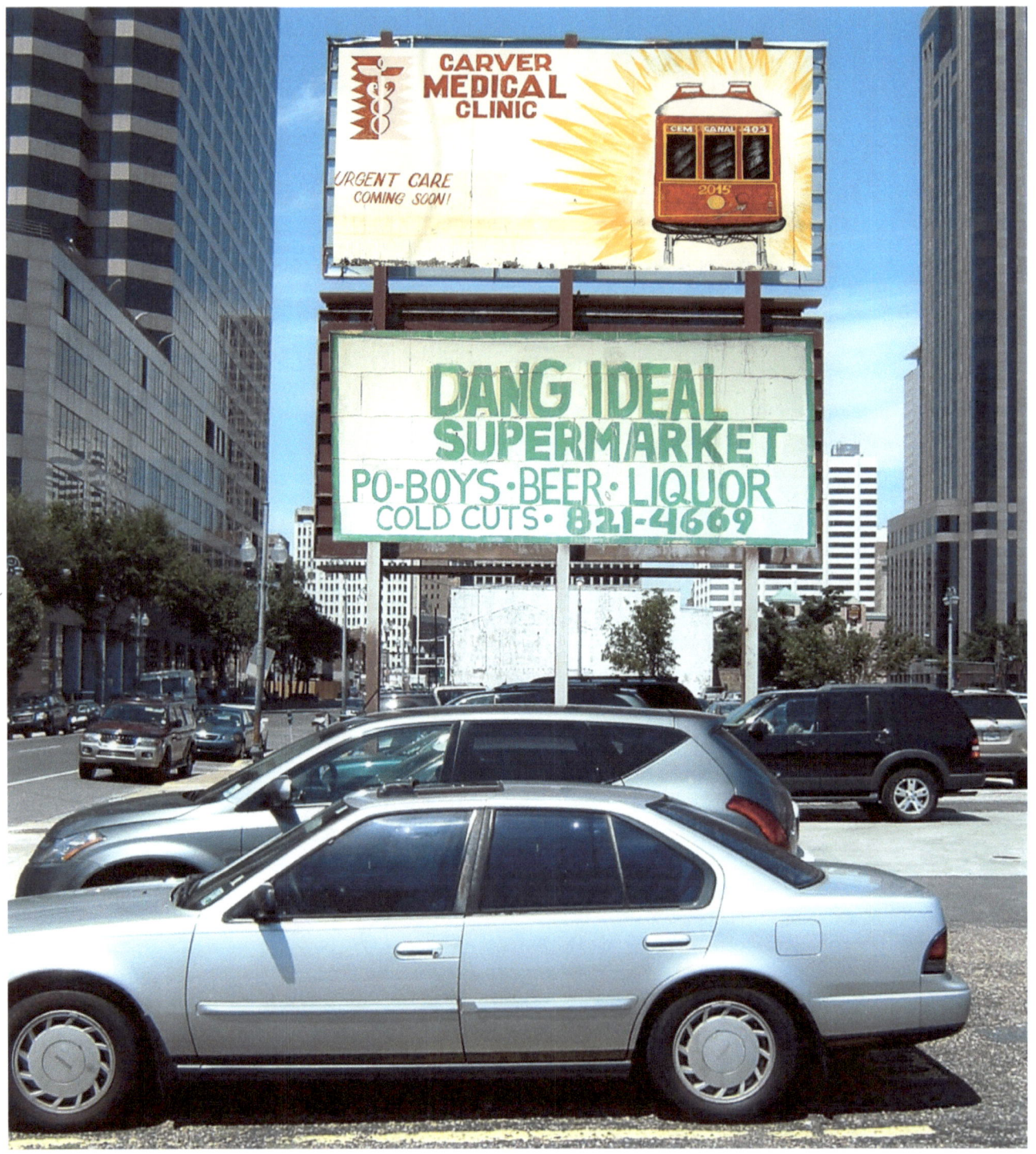

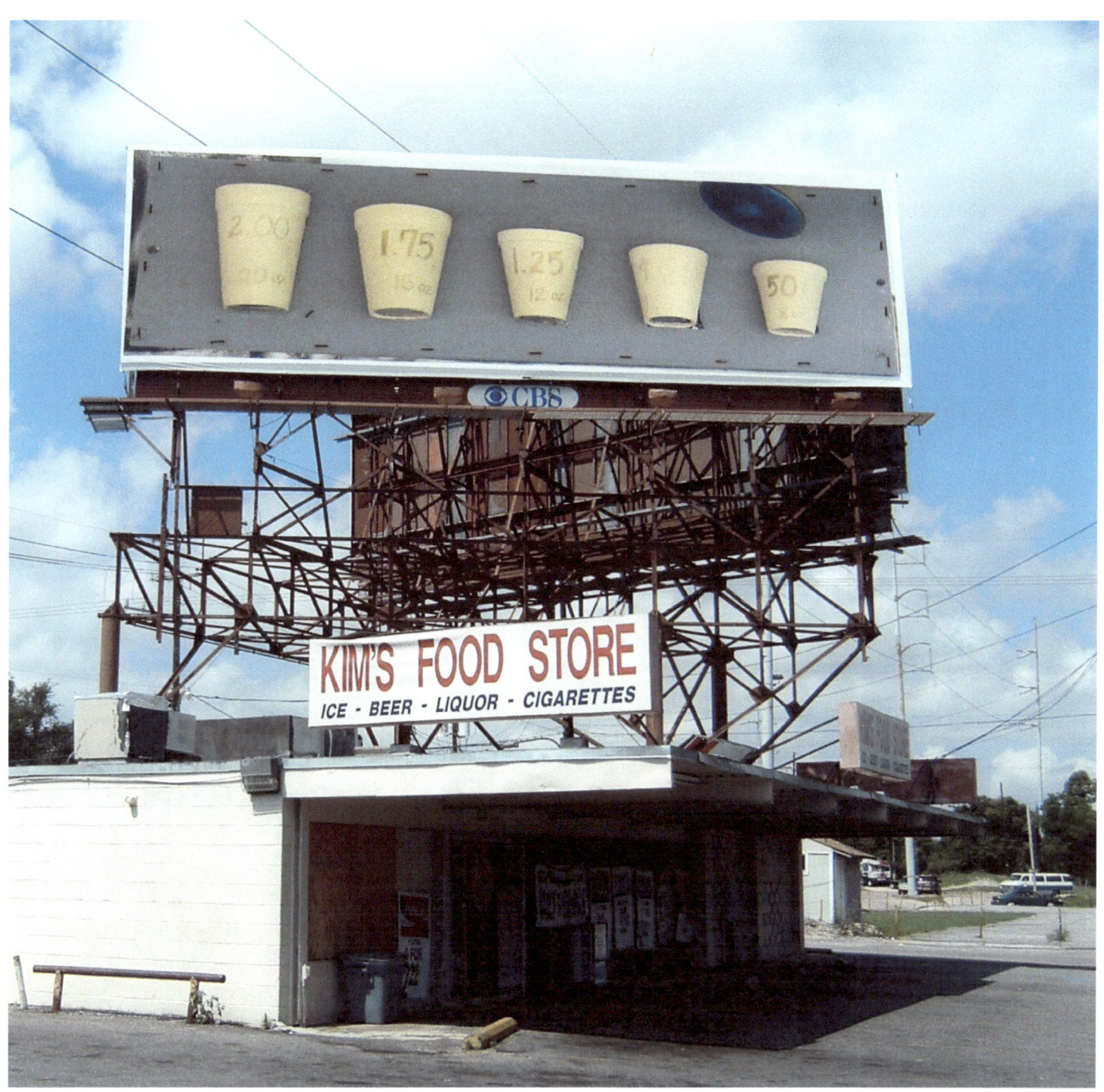

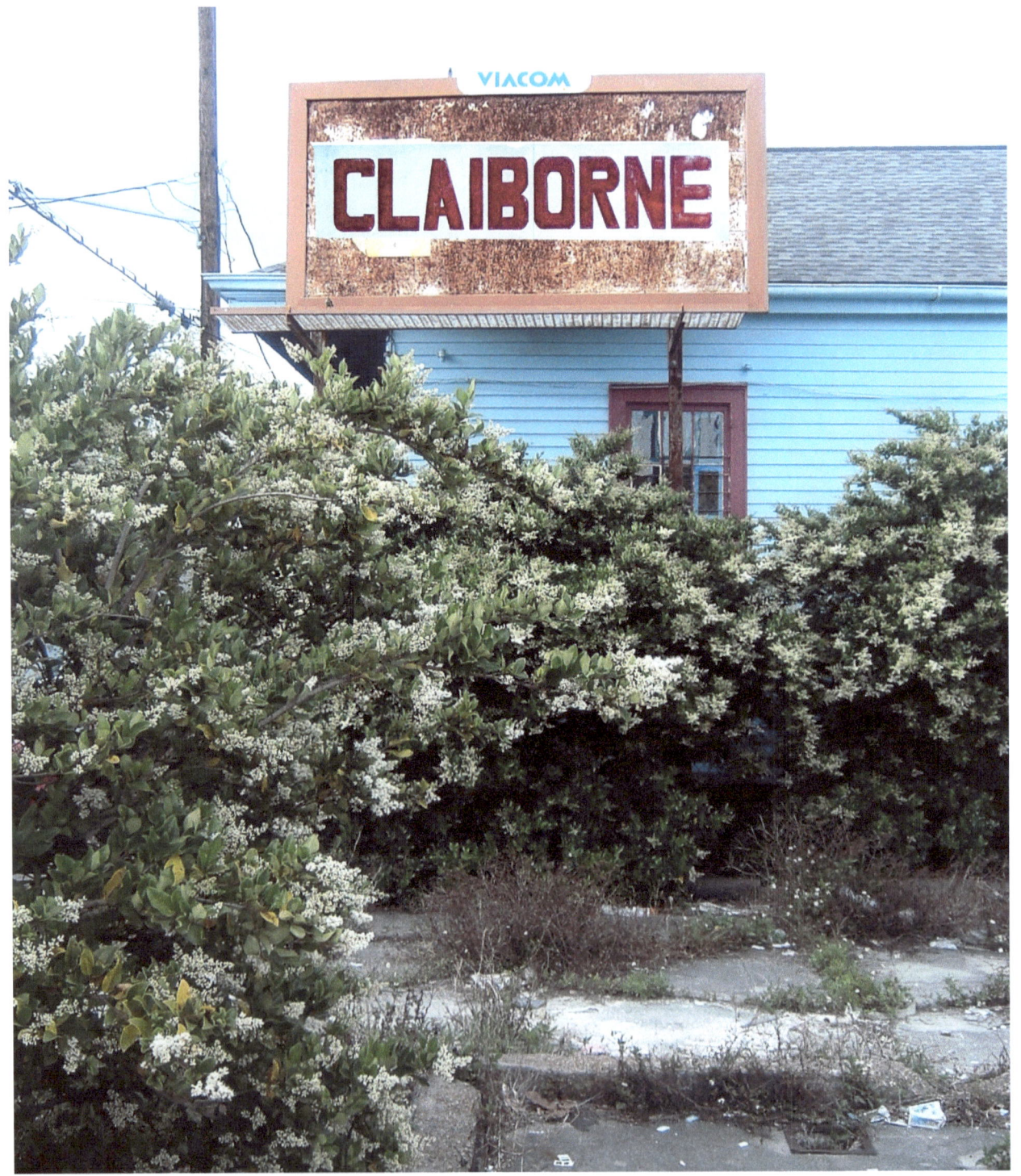

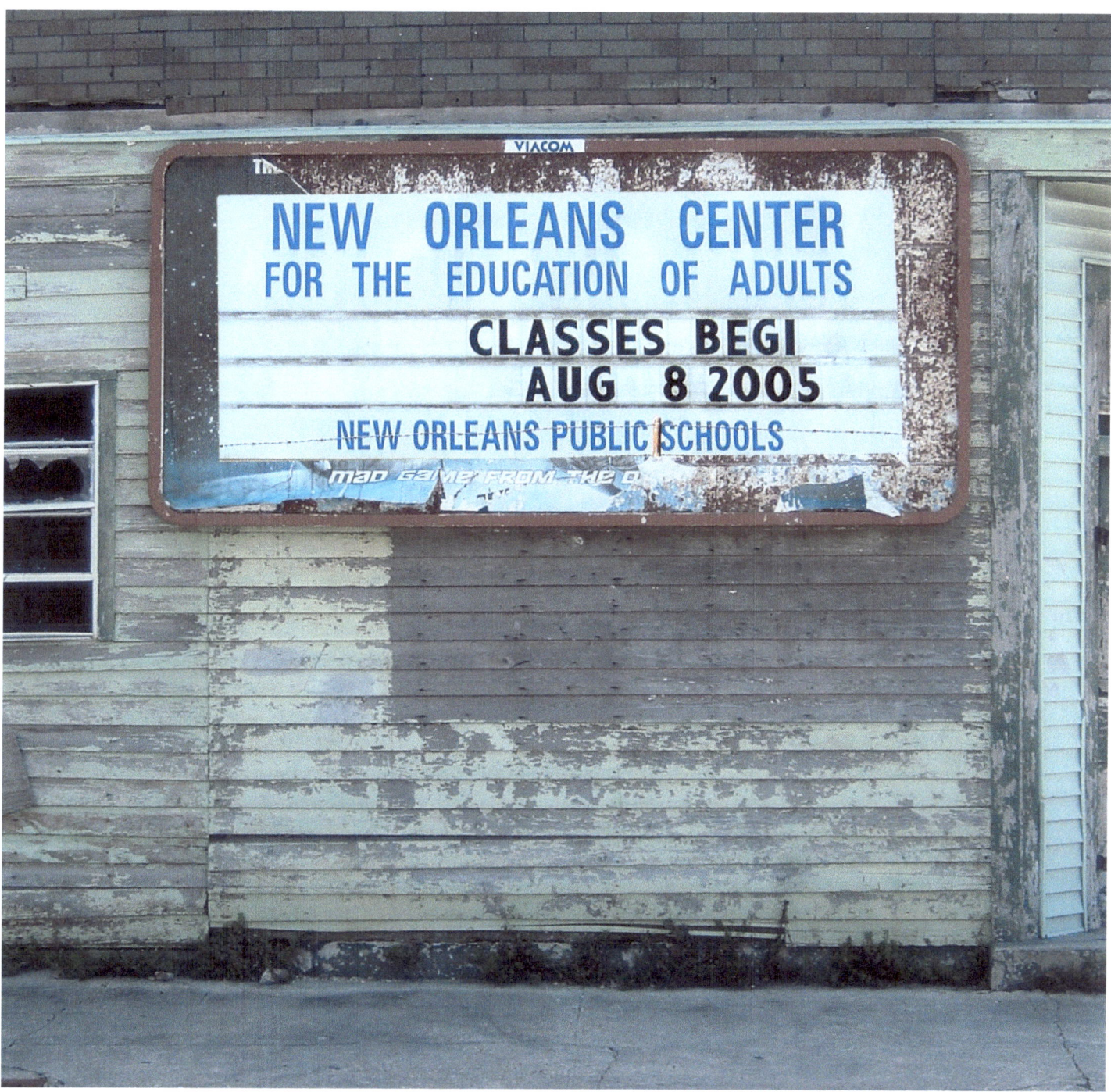

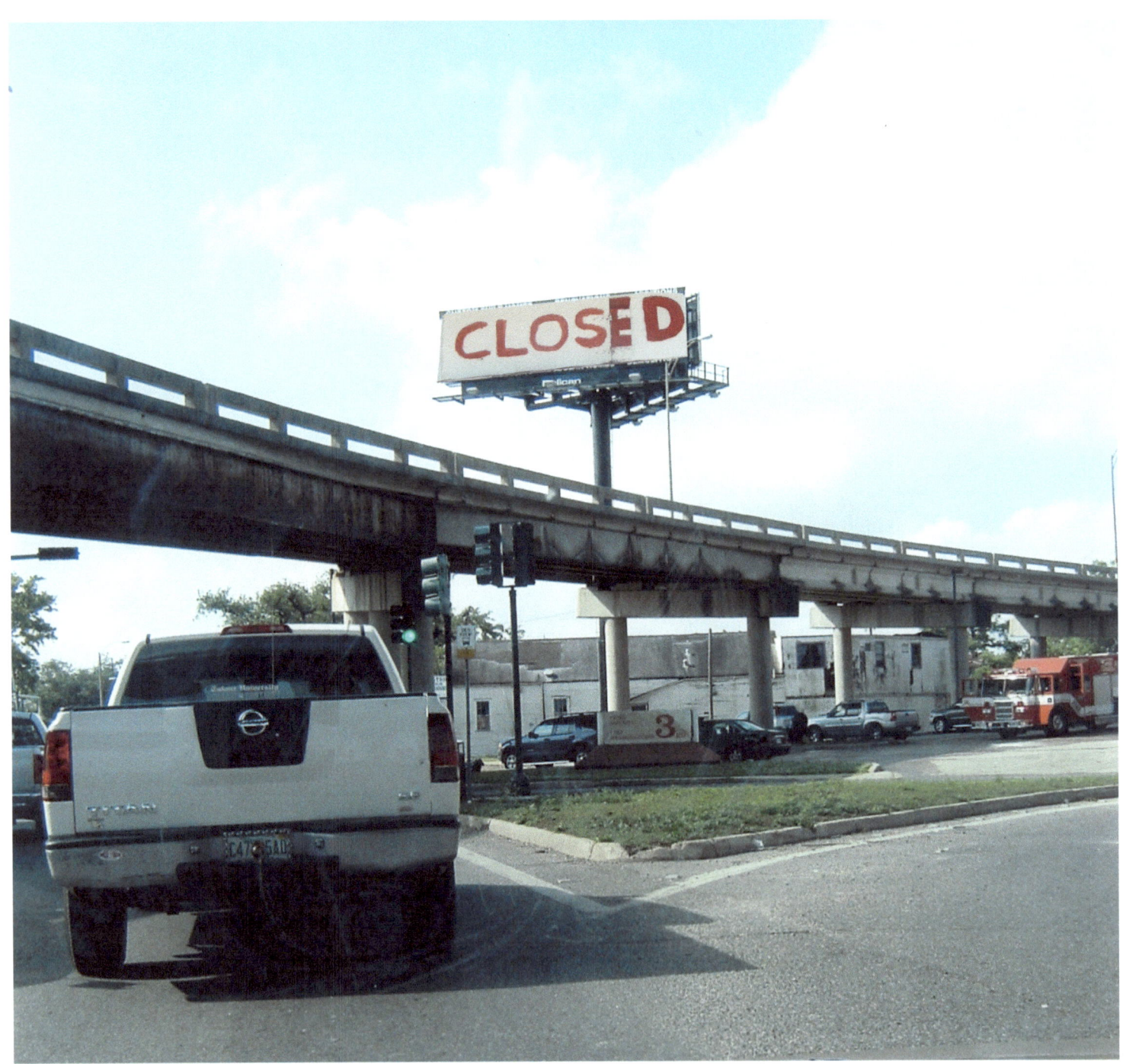

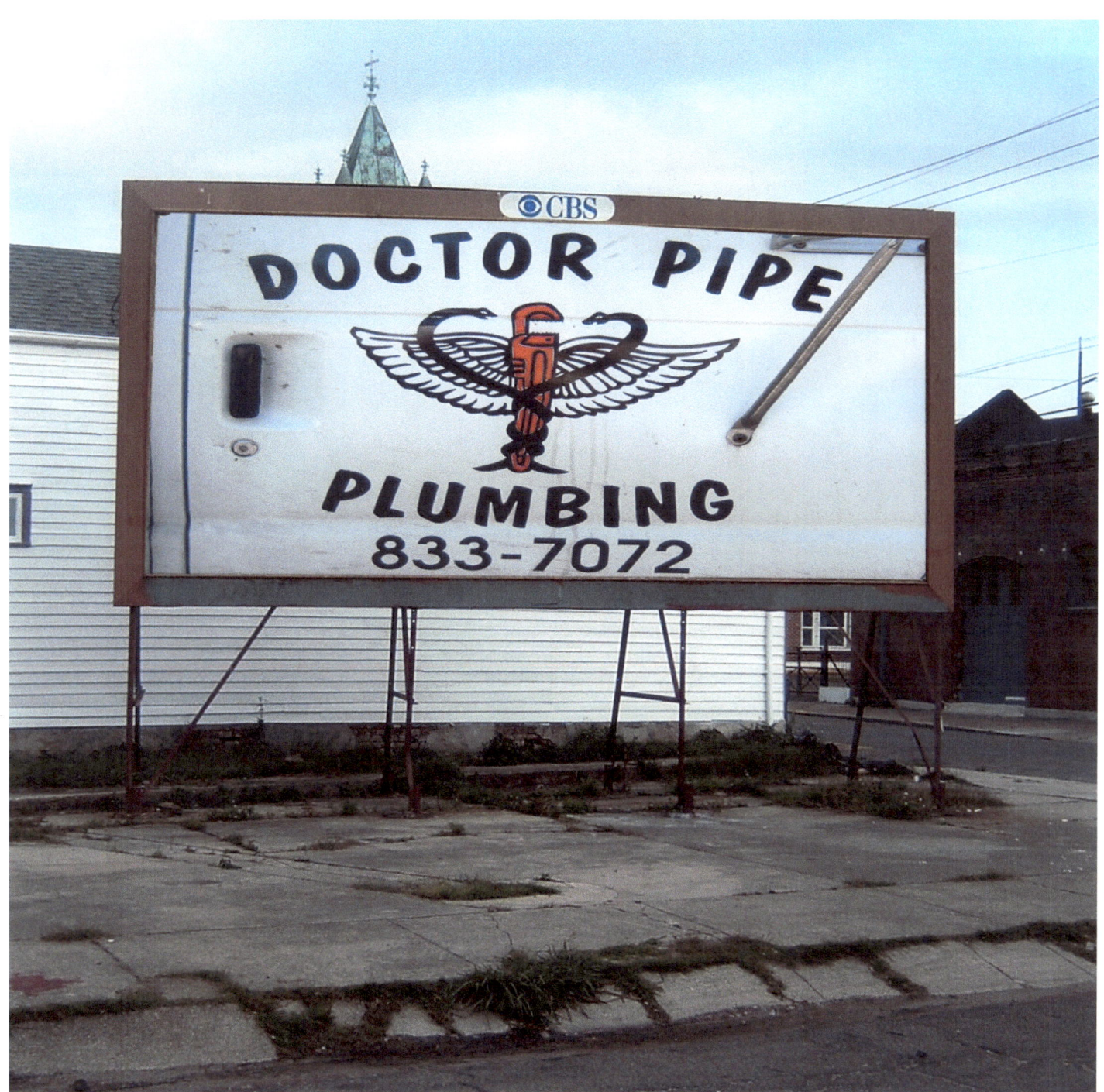

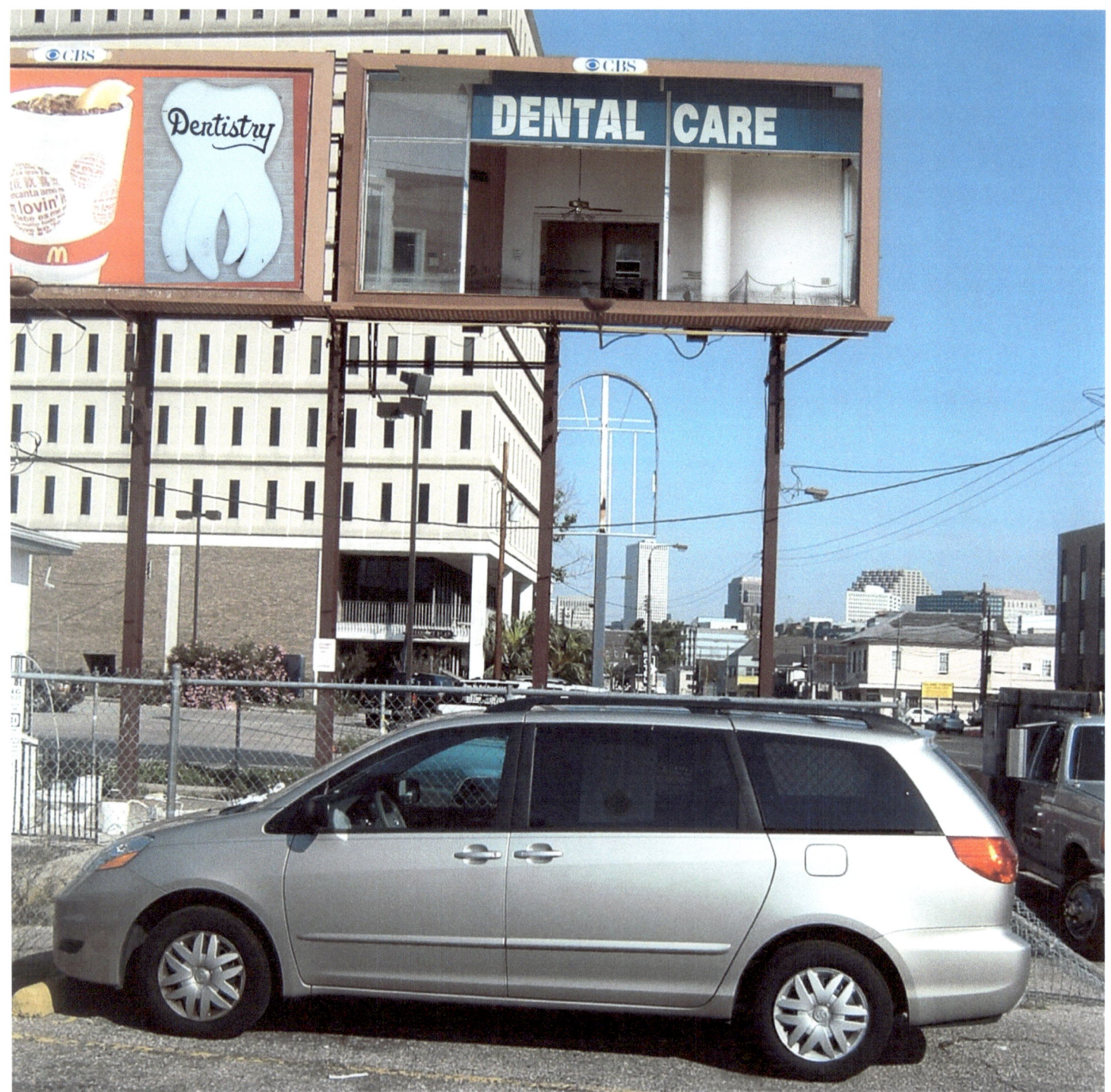

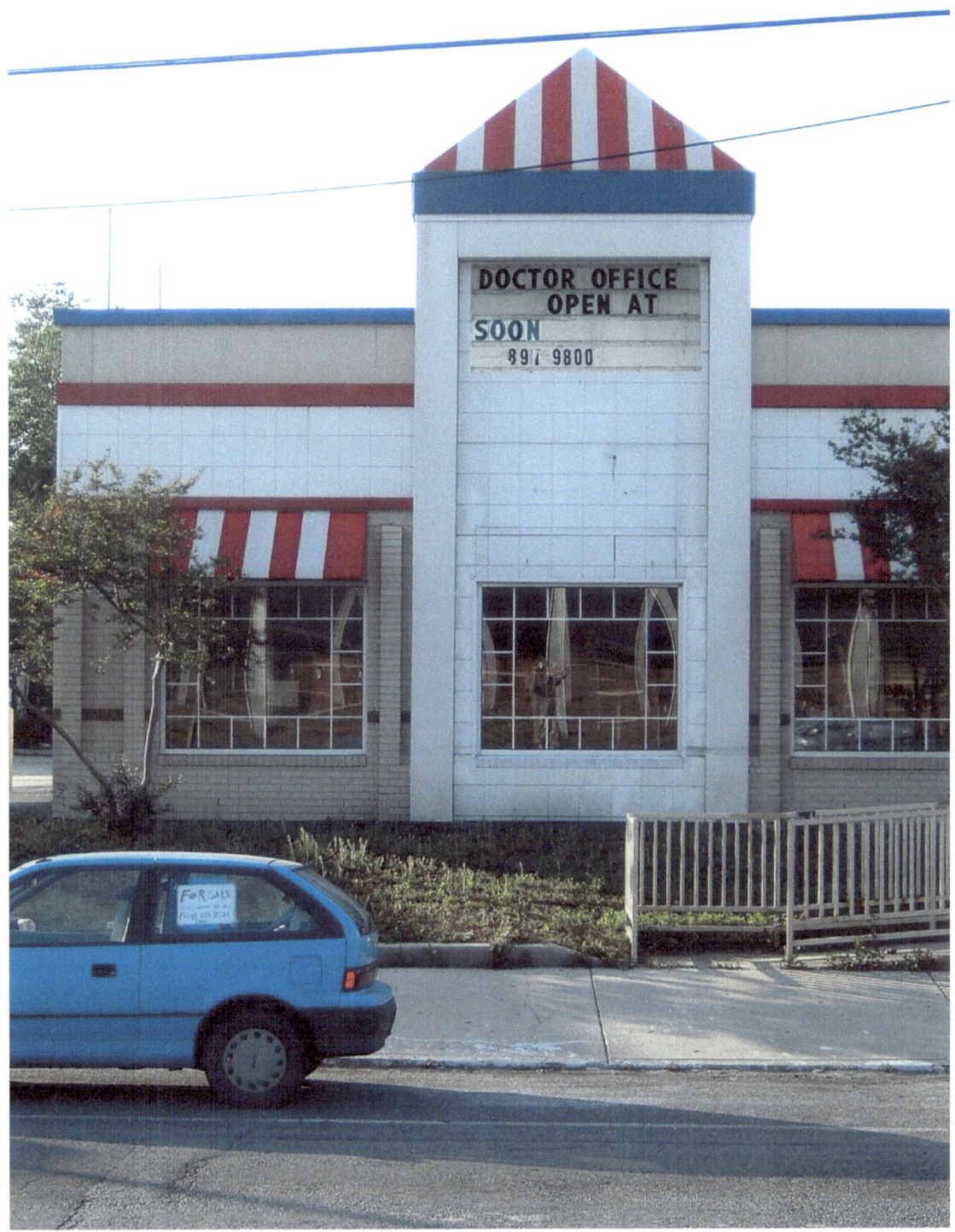

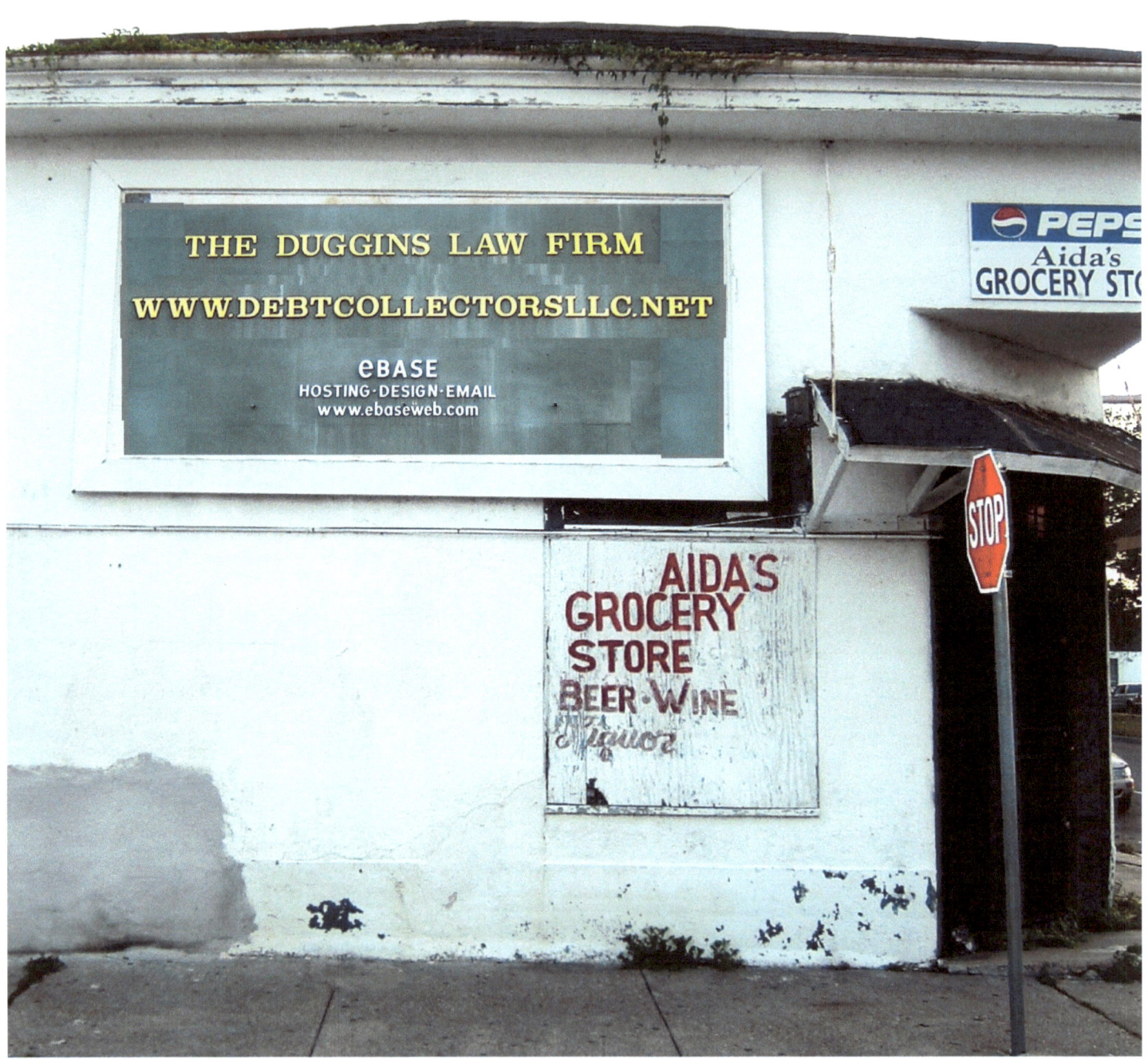

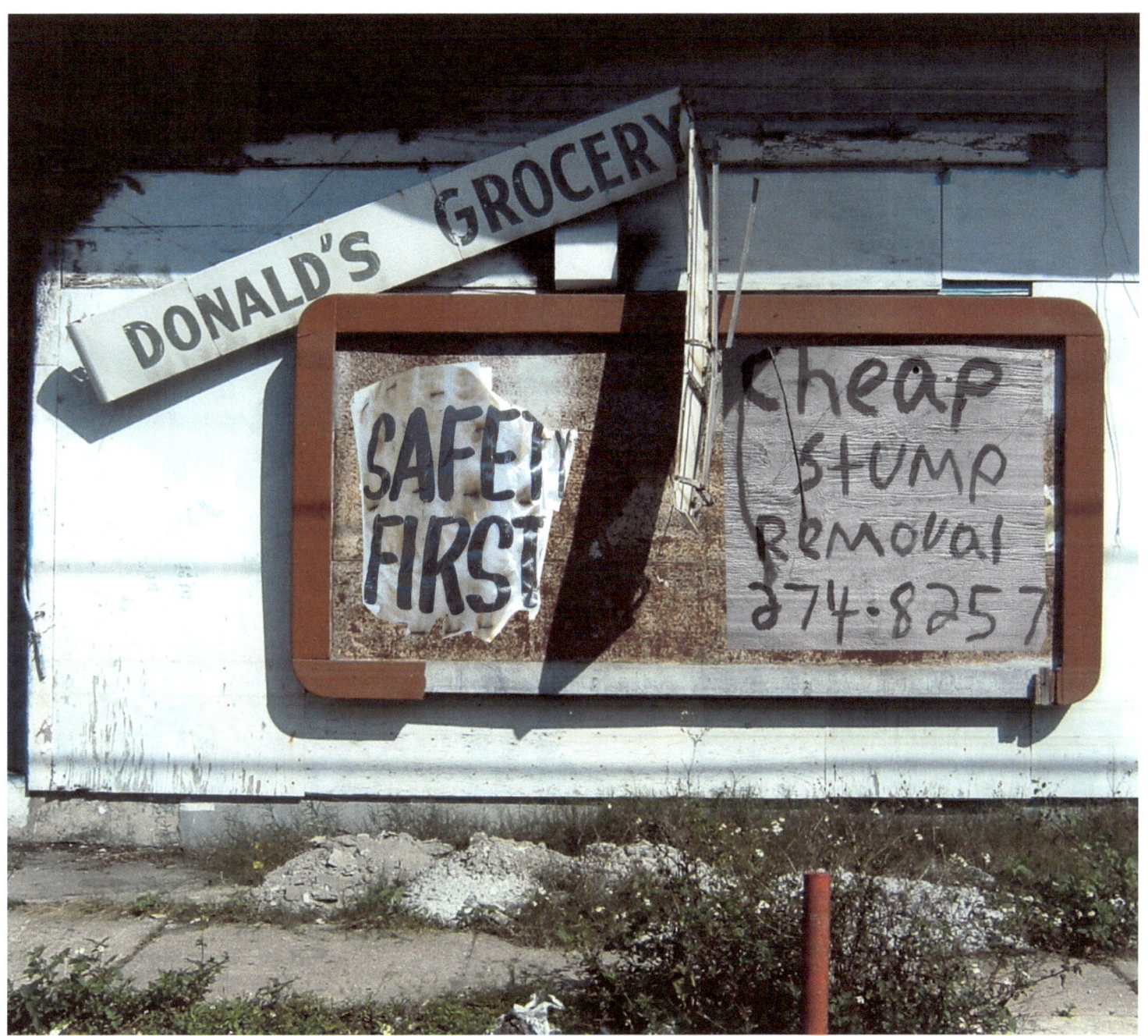

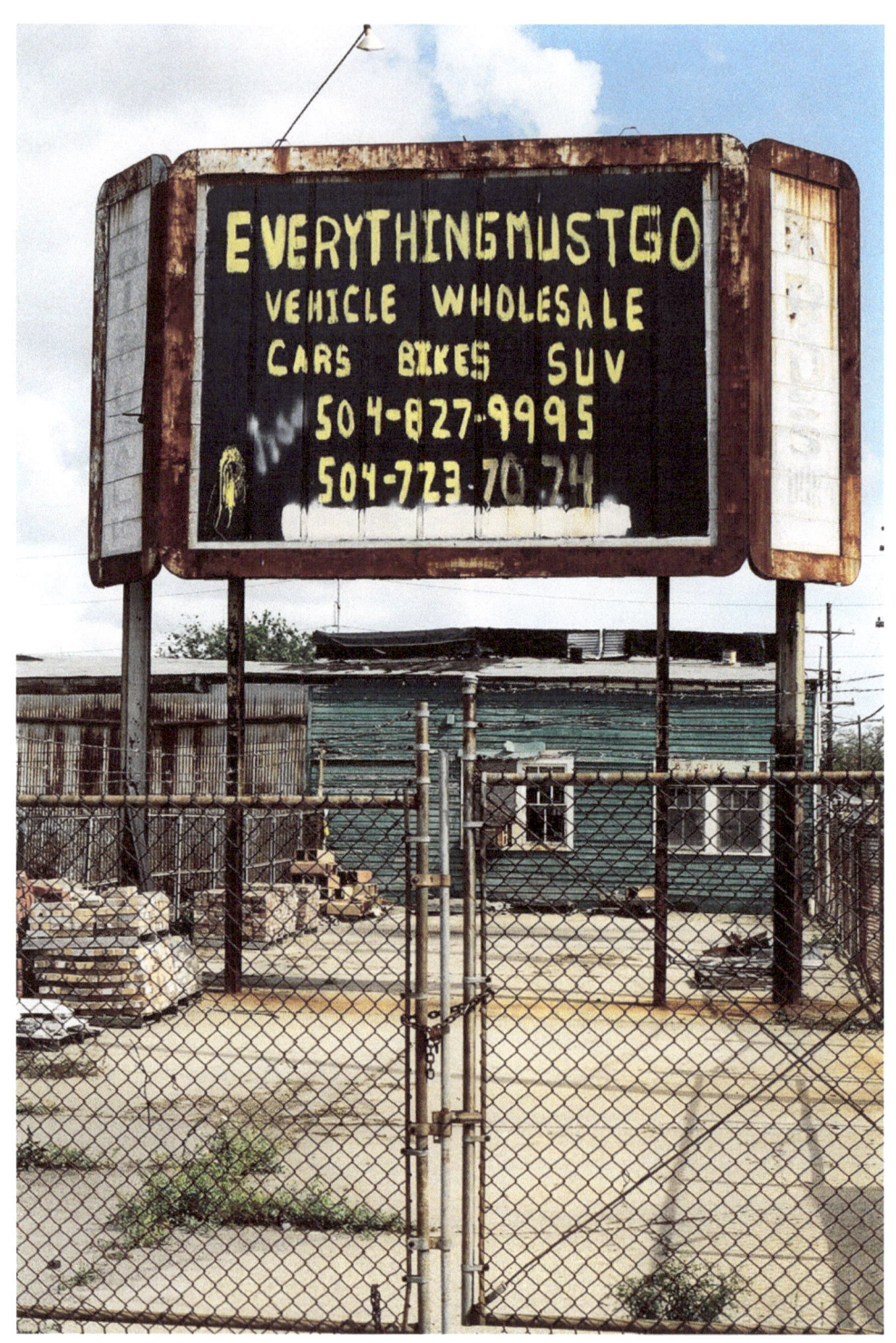

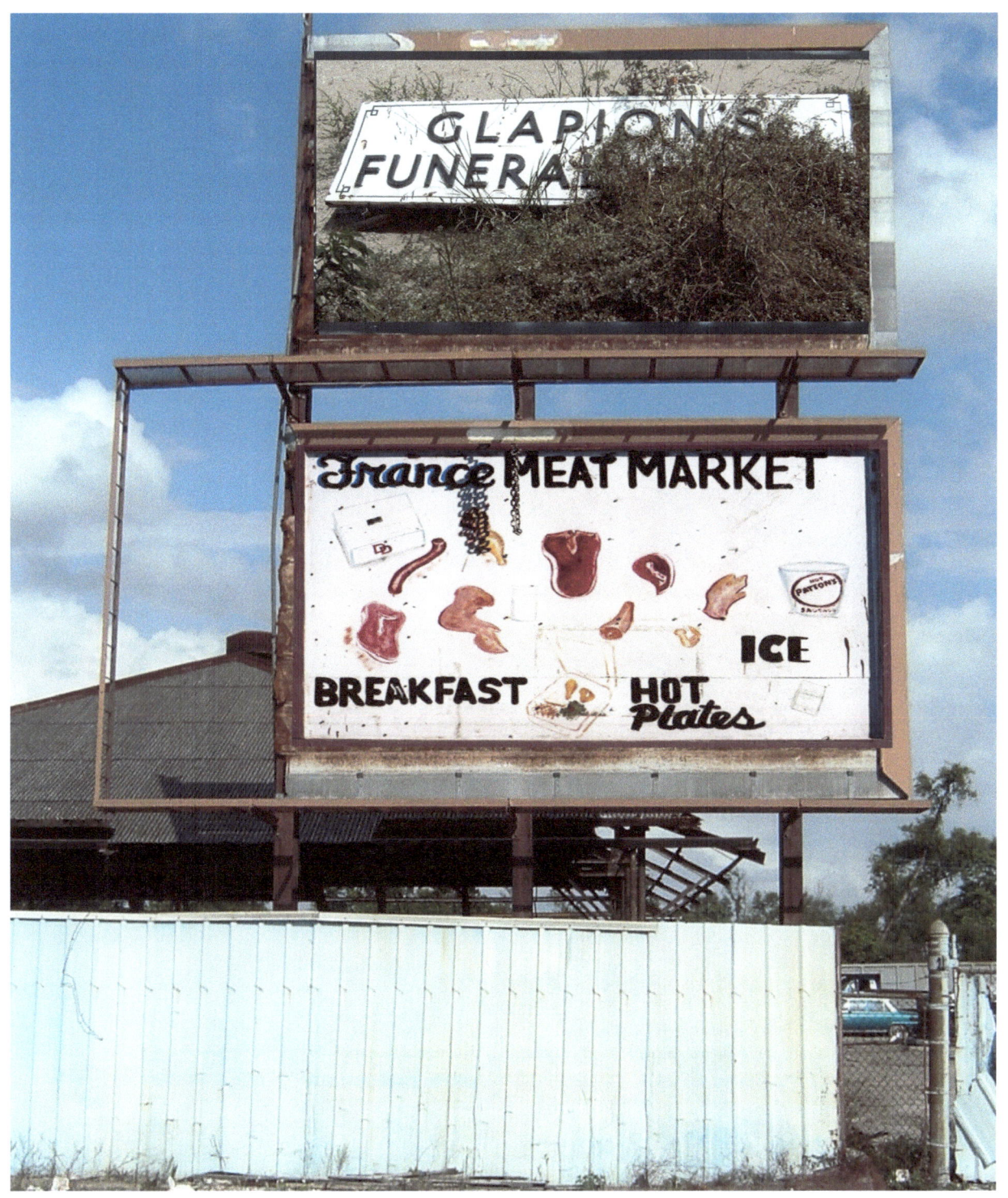

27

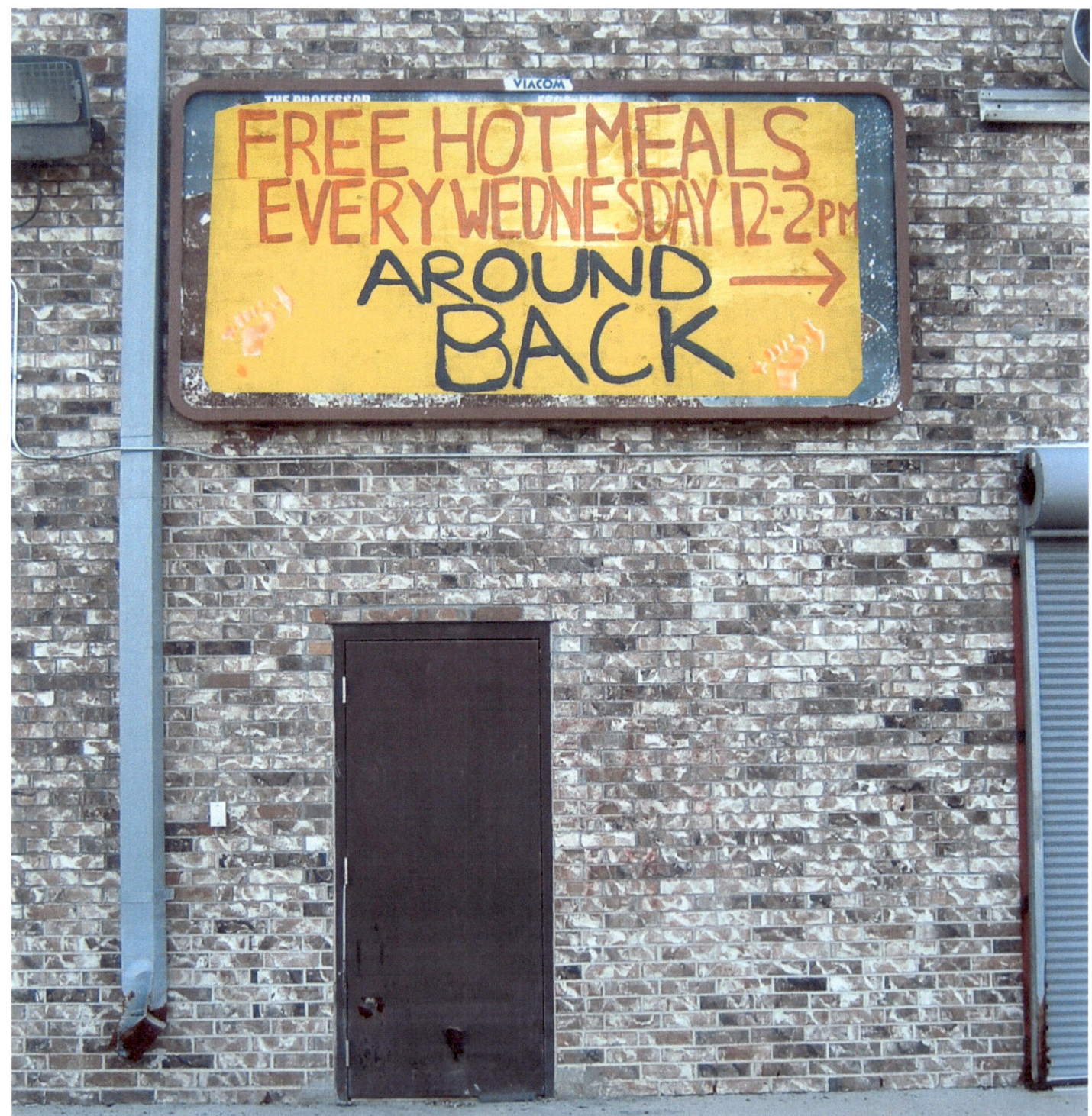

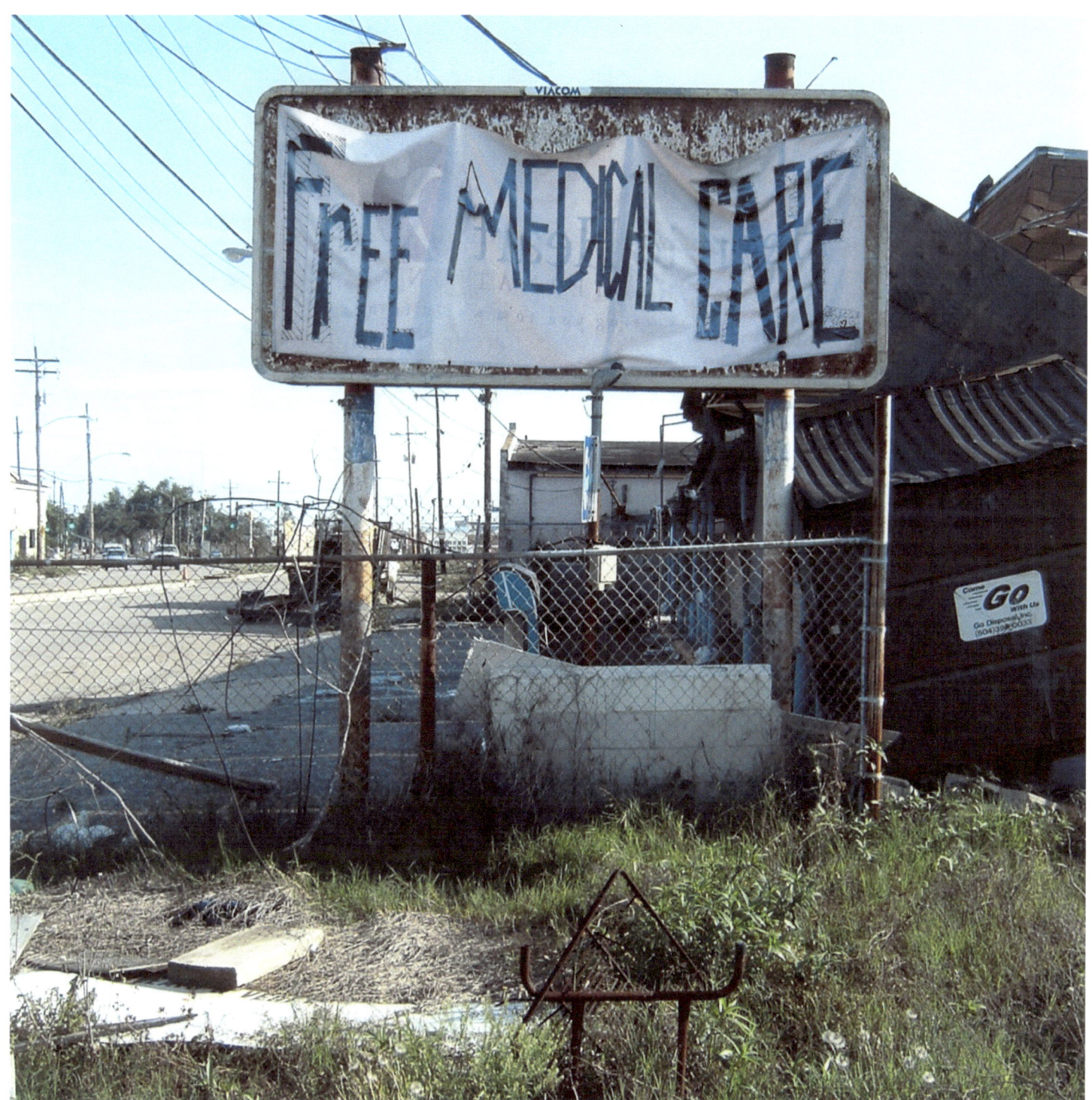

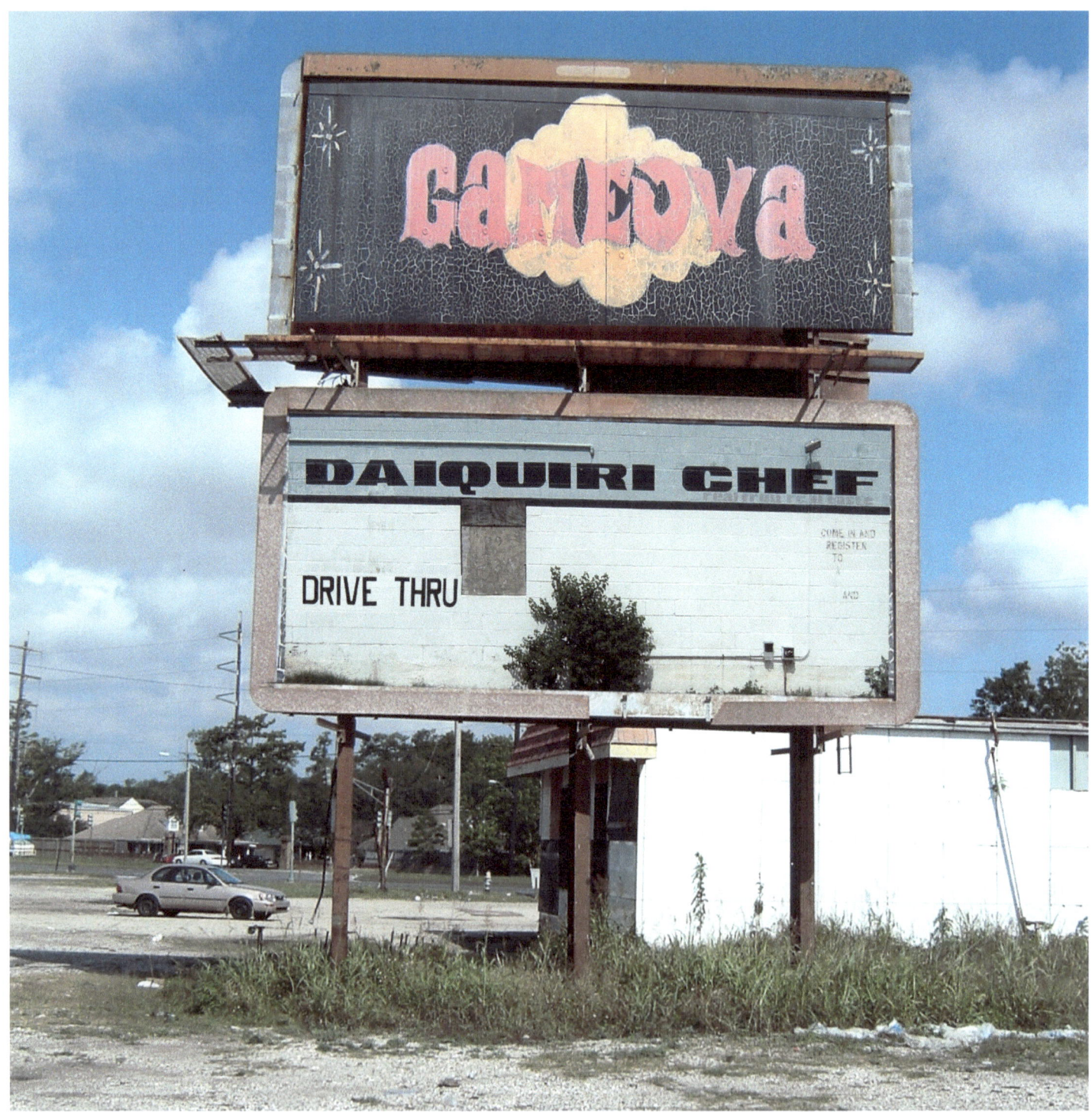

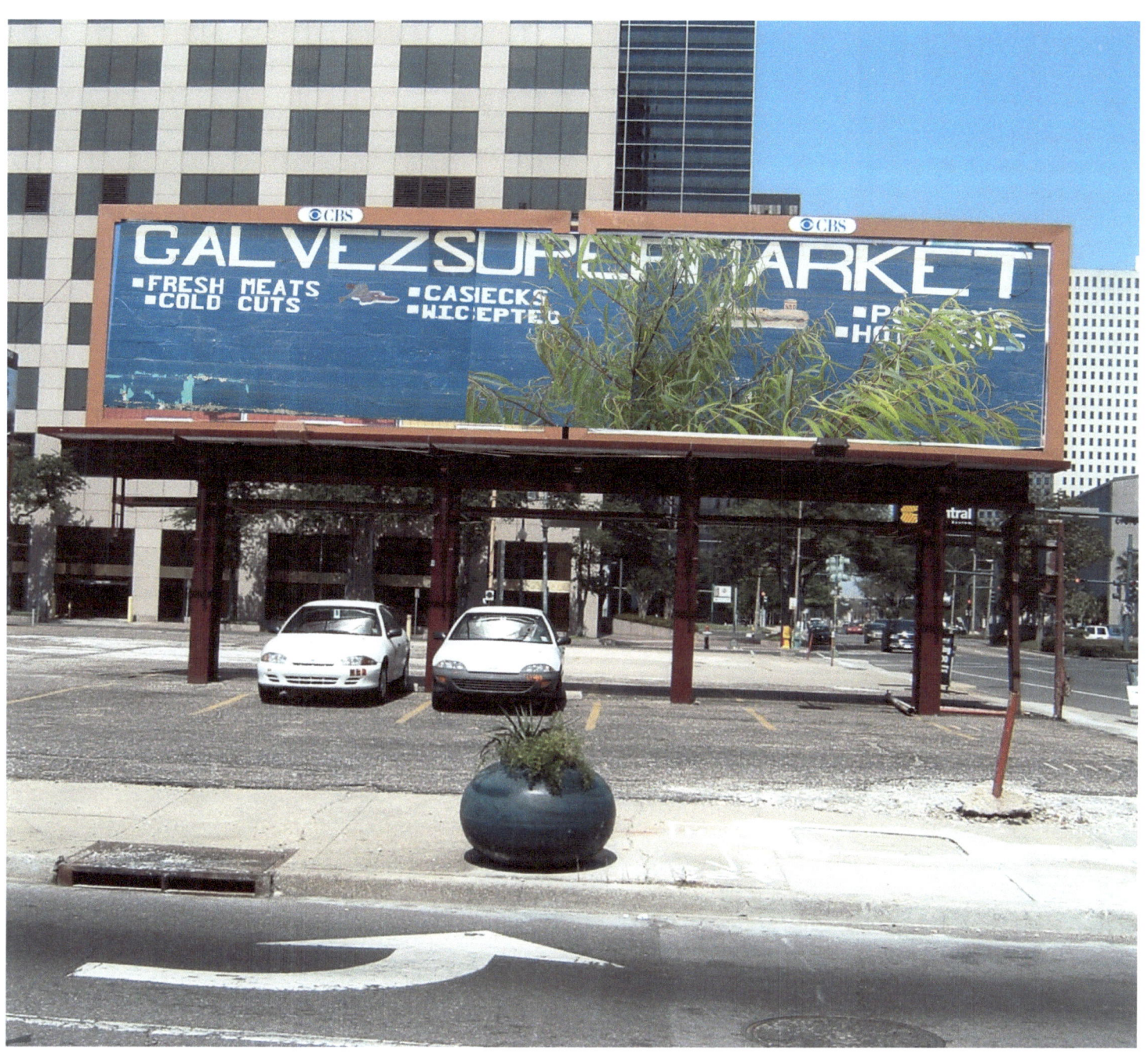

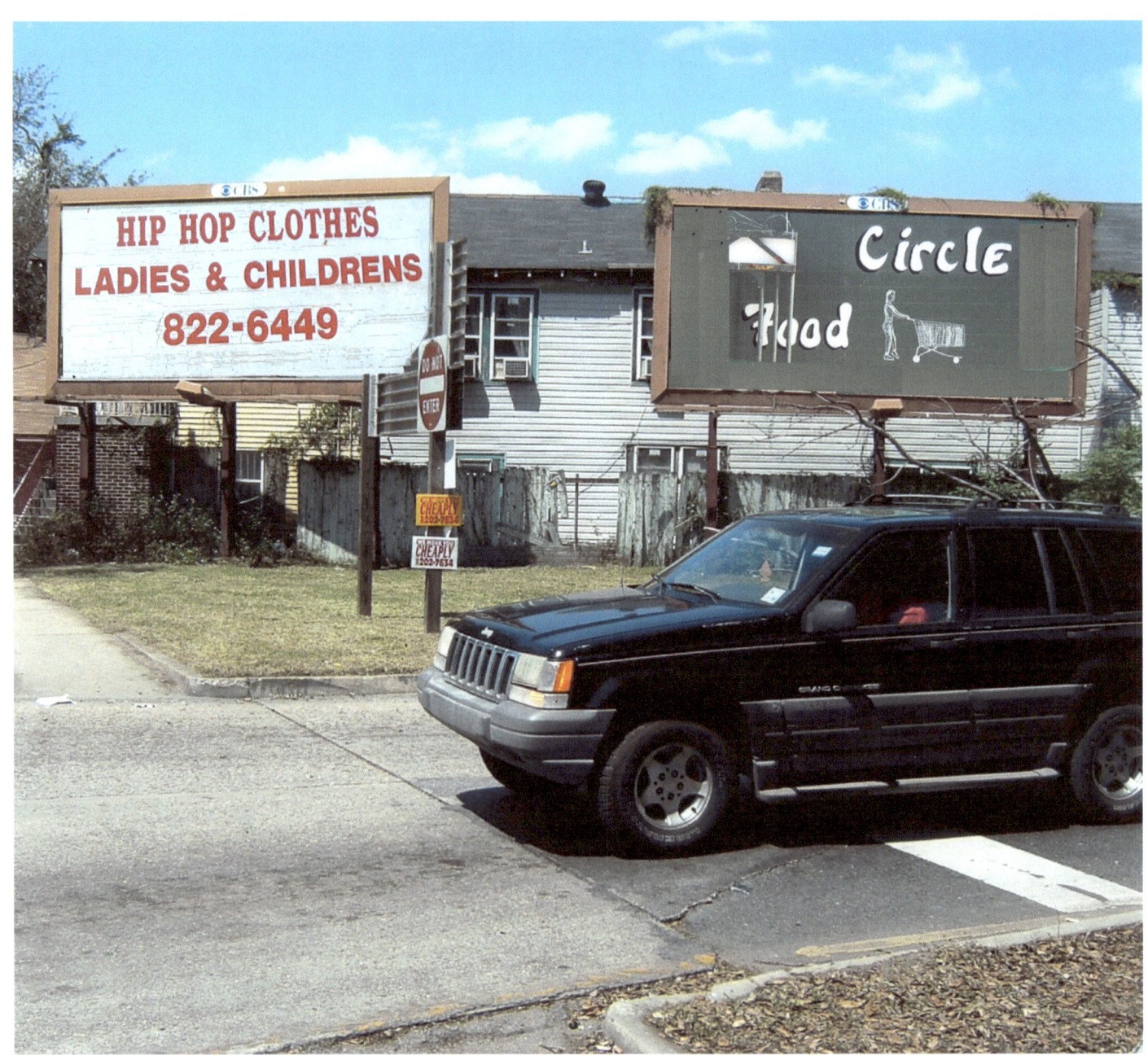

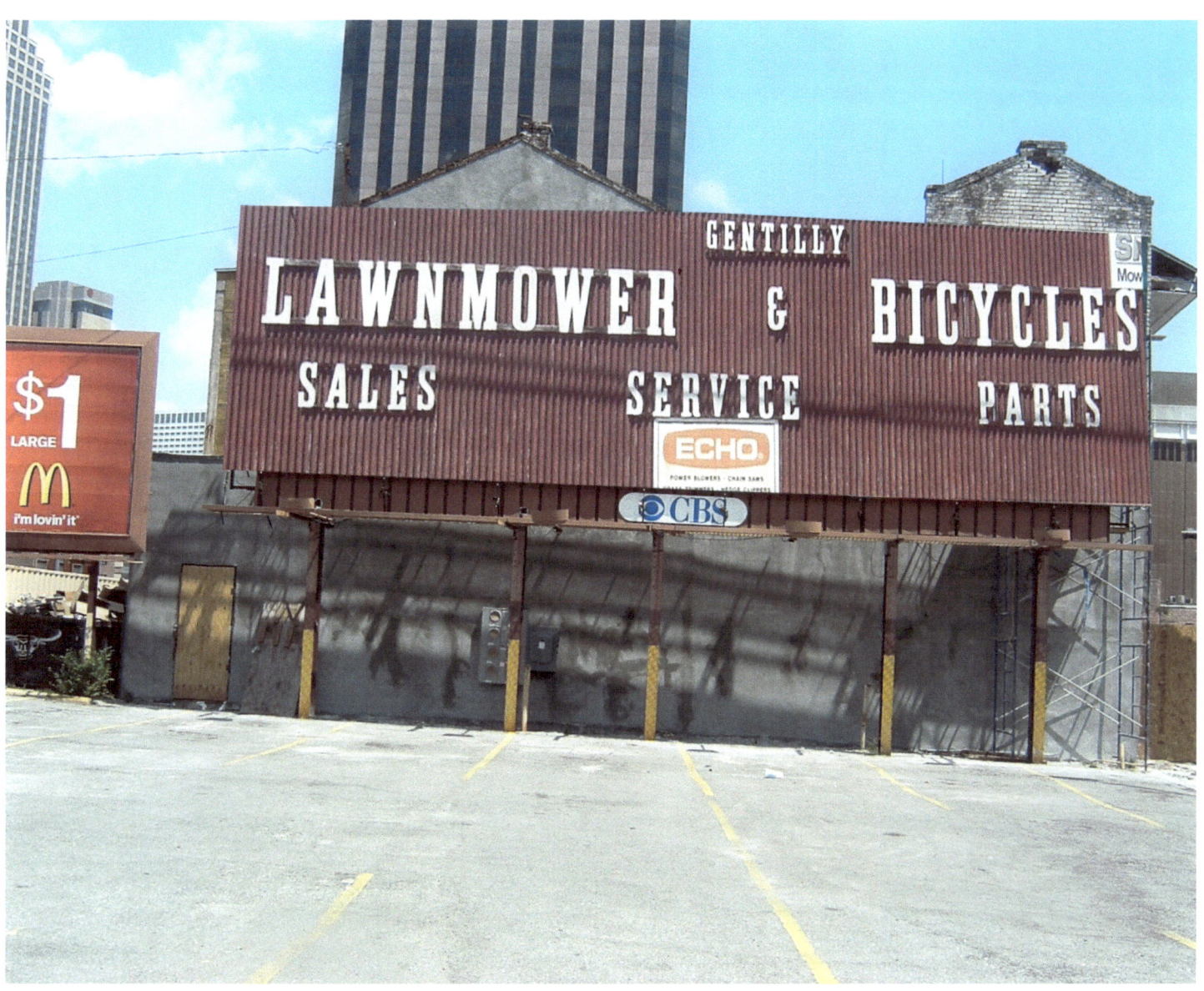

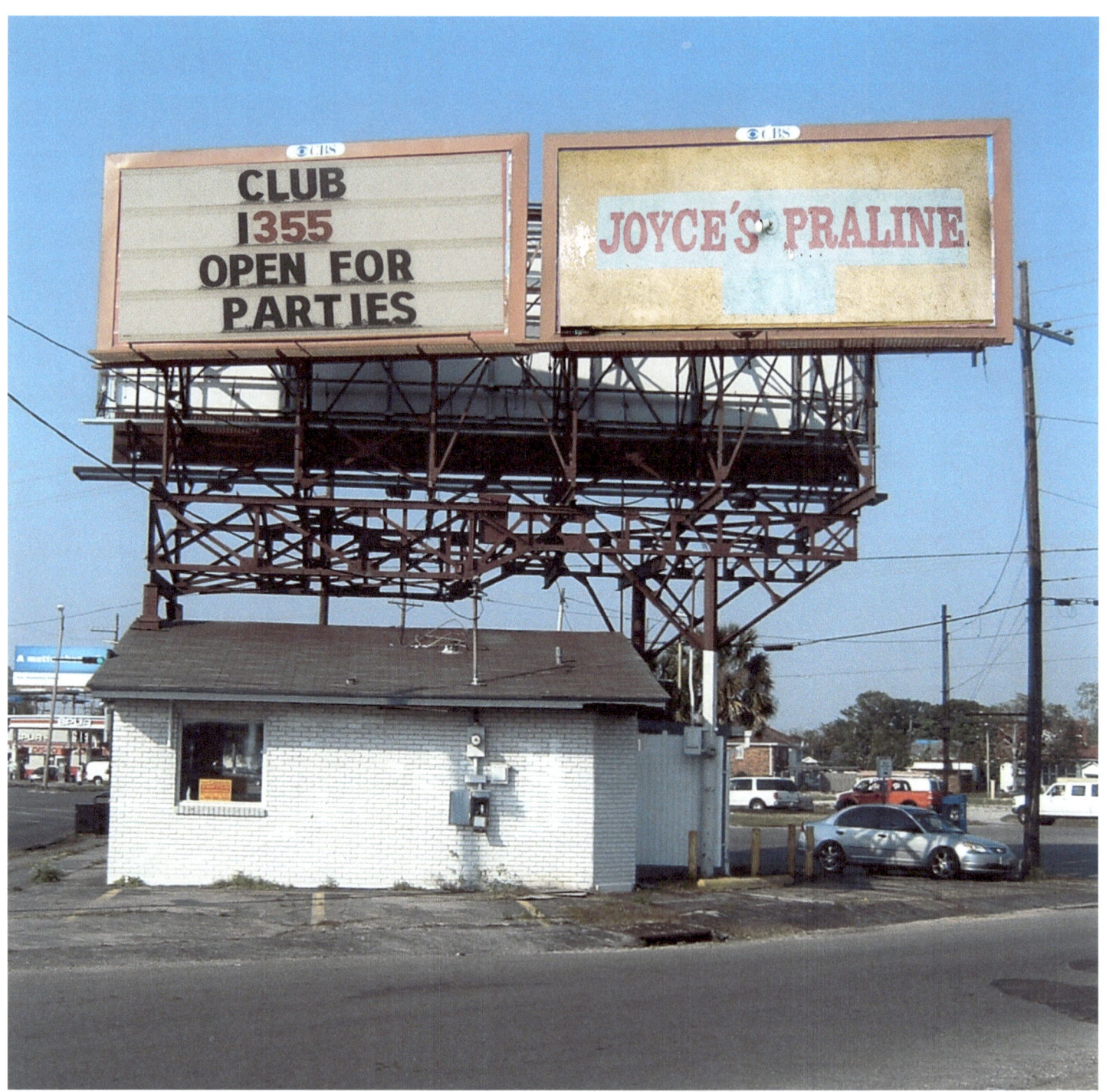

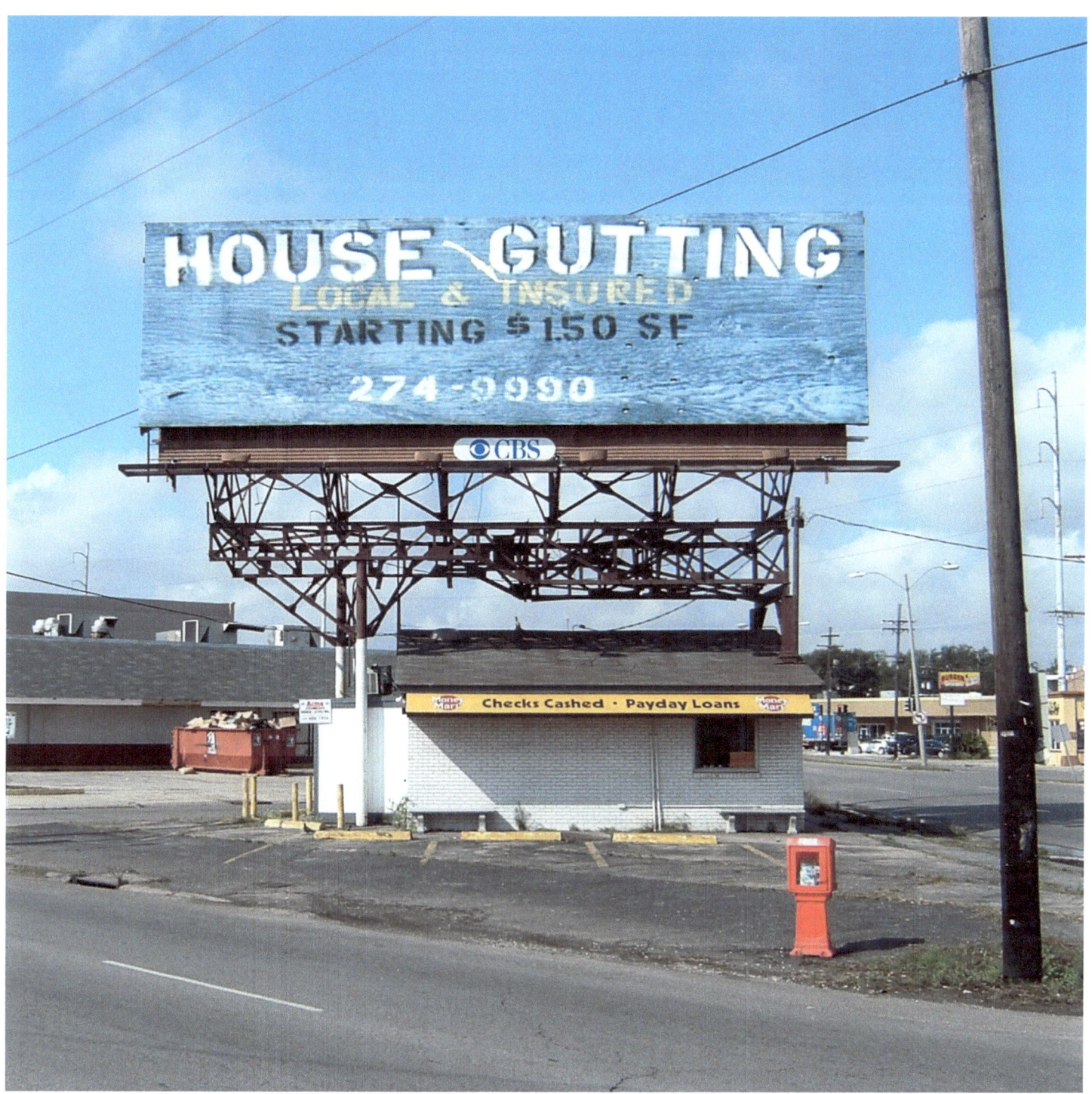

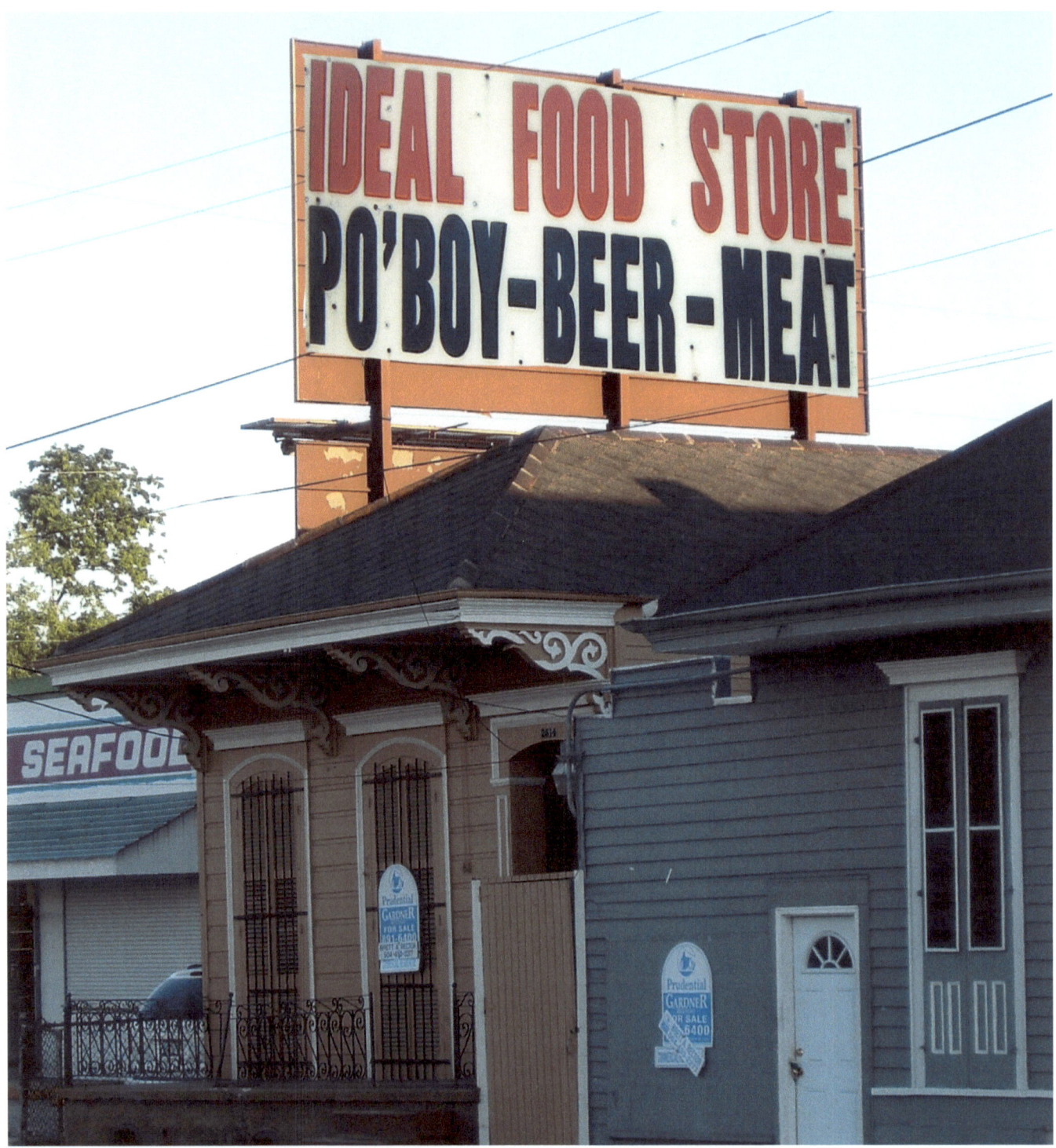

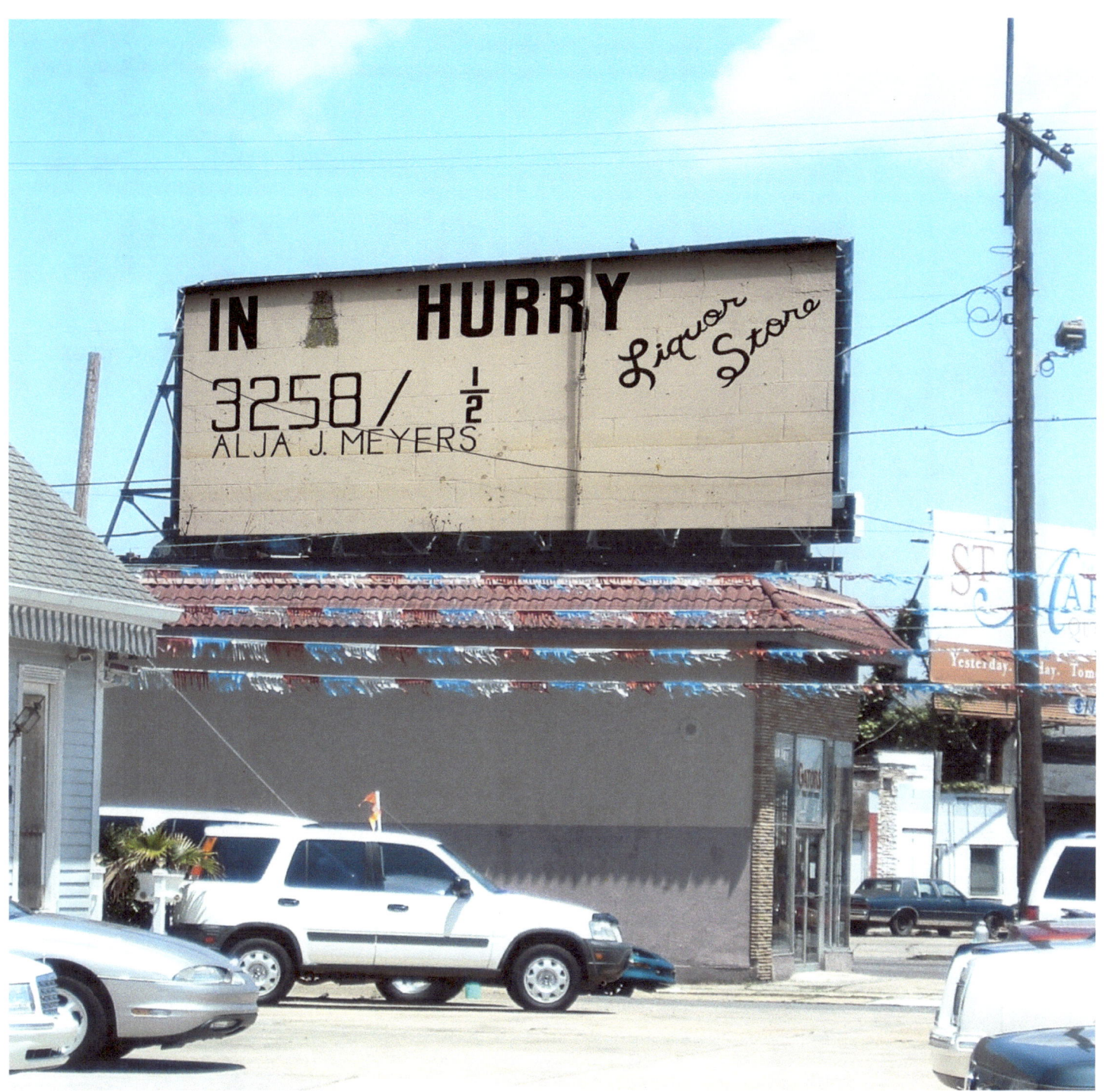

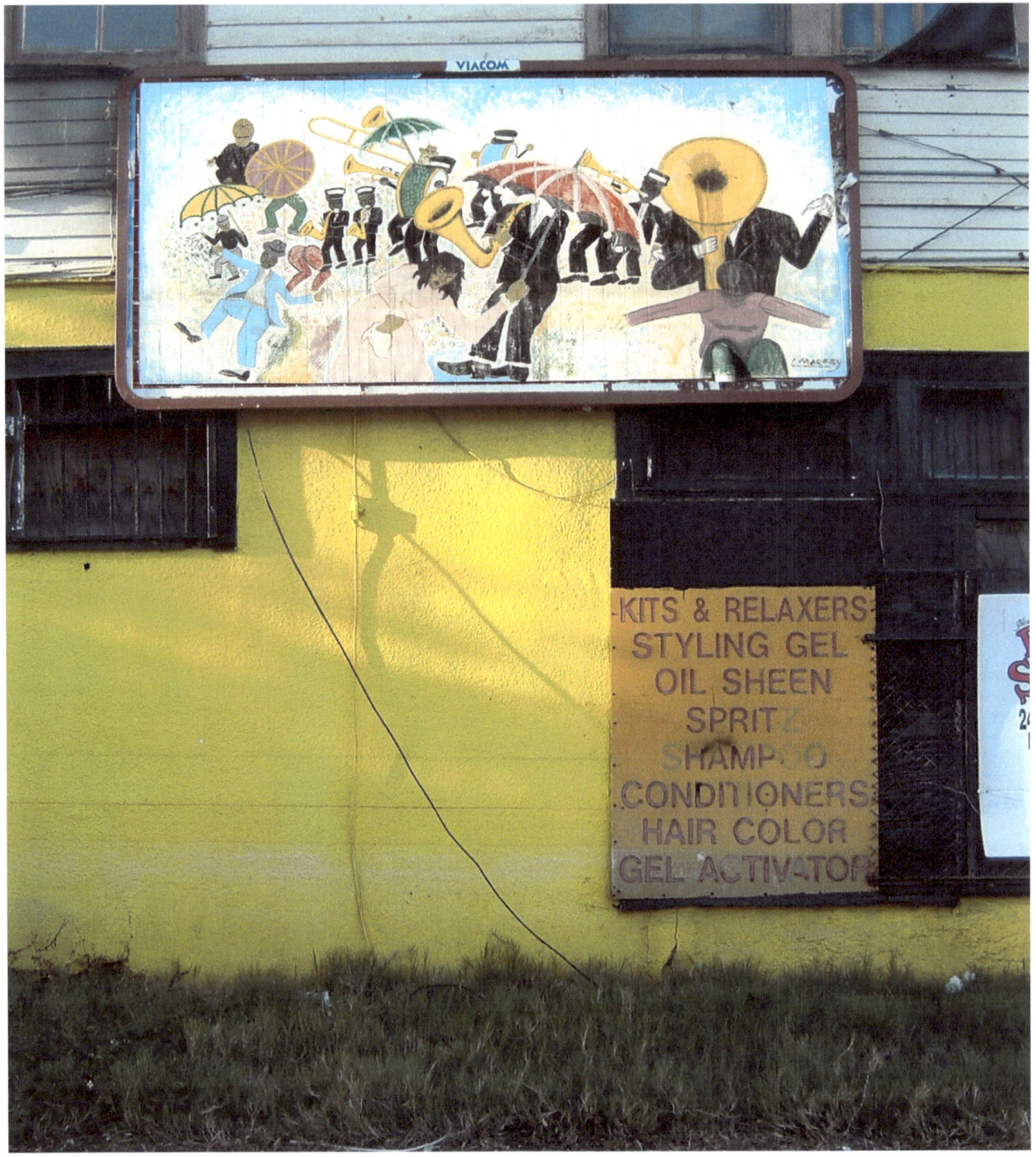

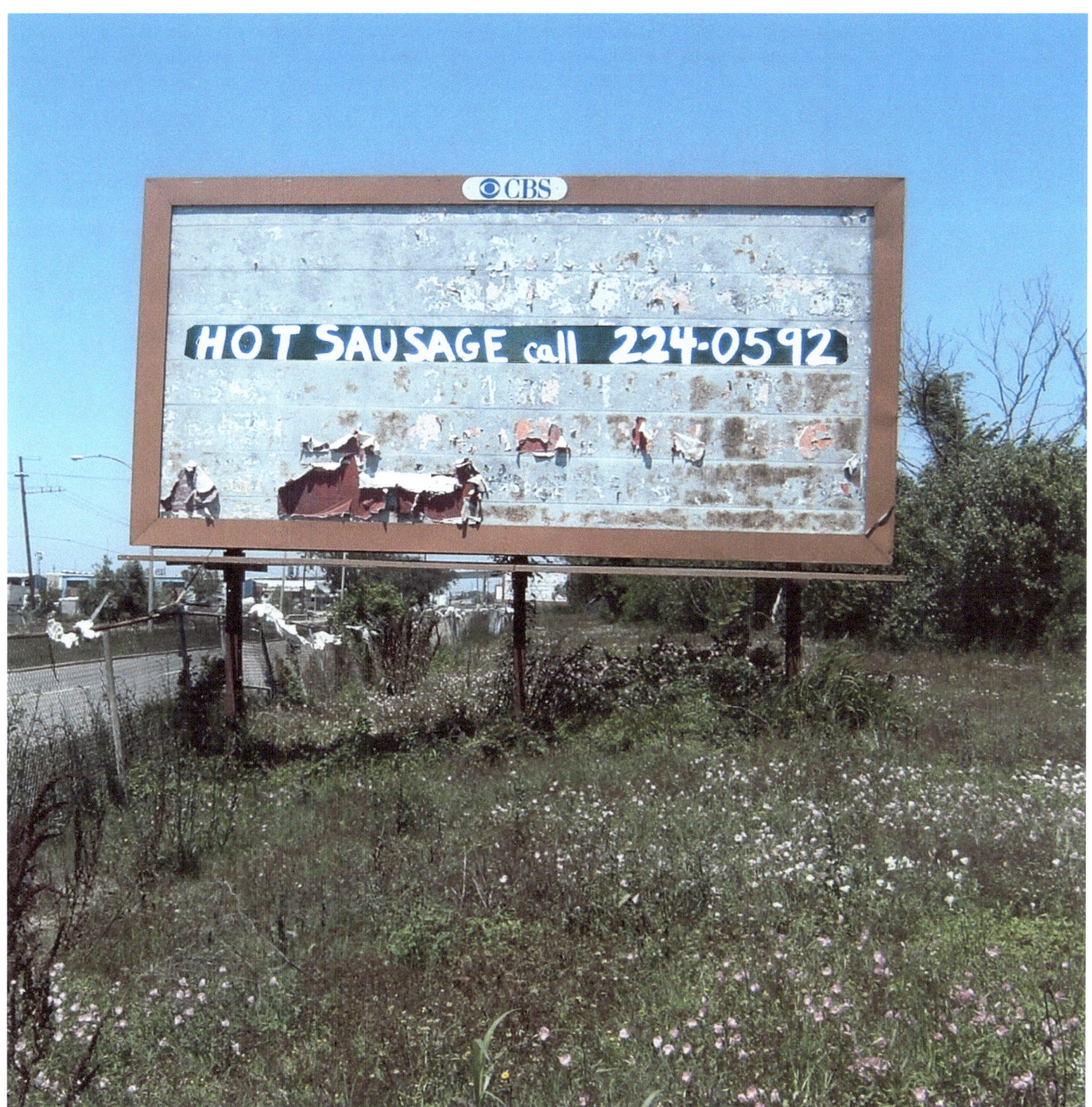

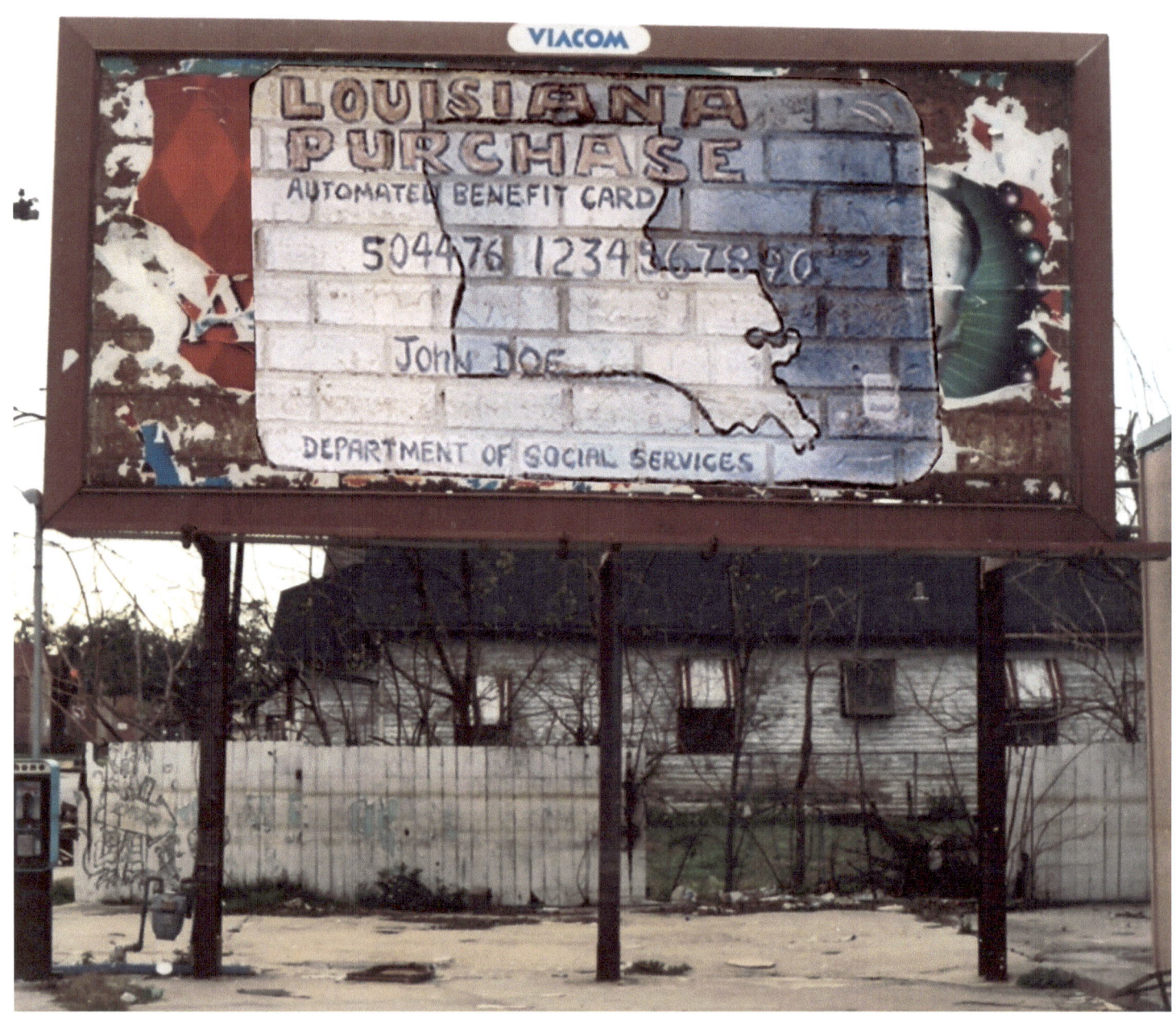

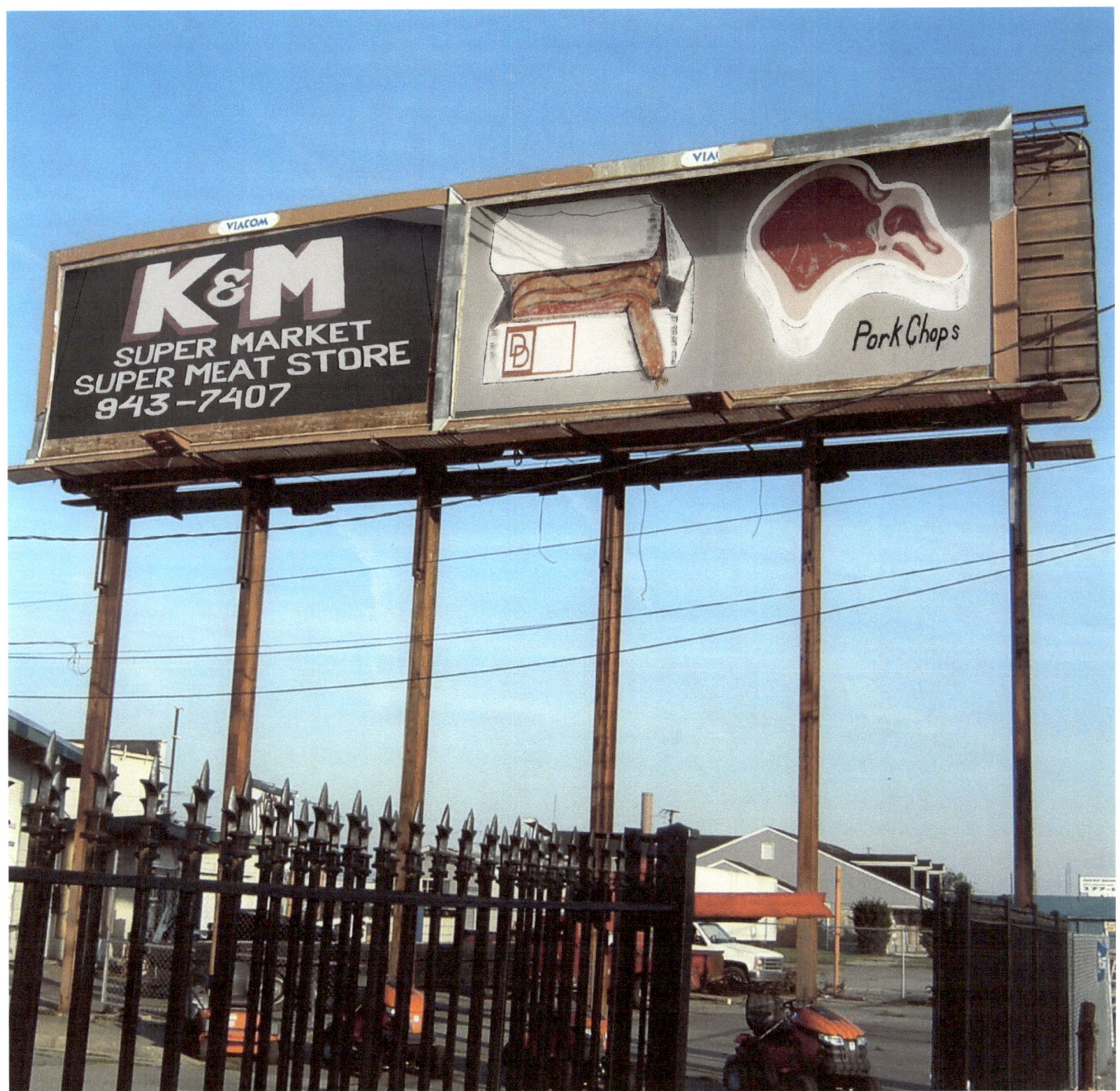

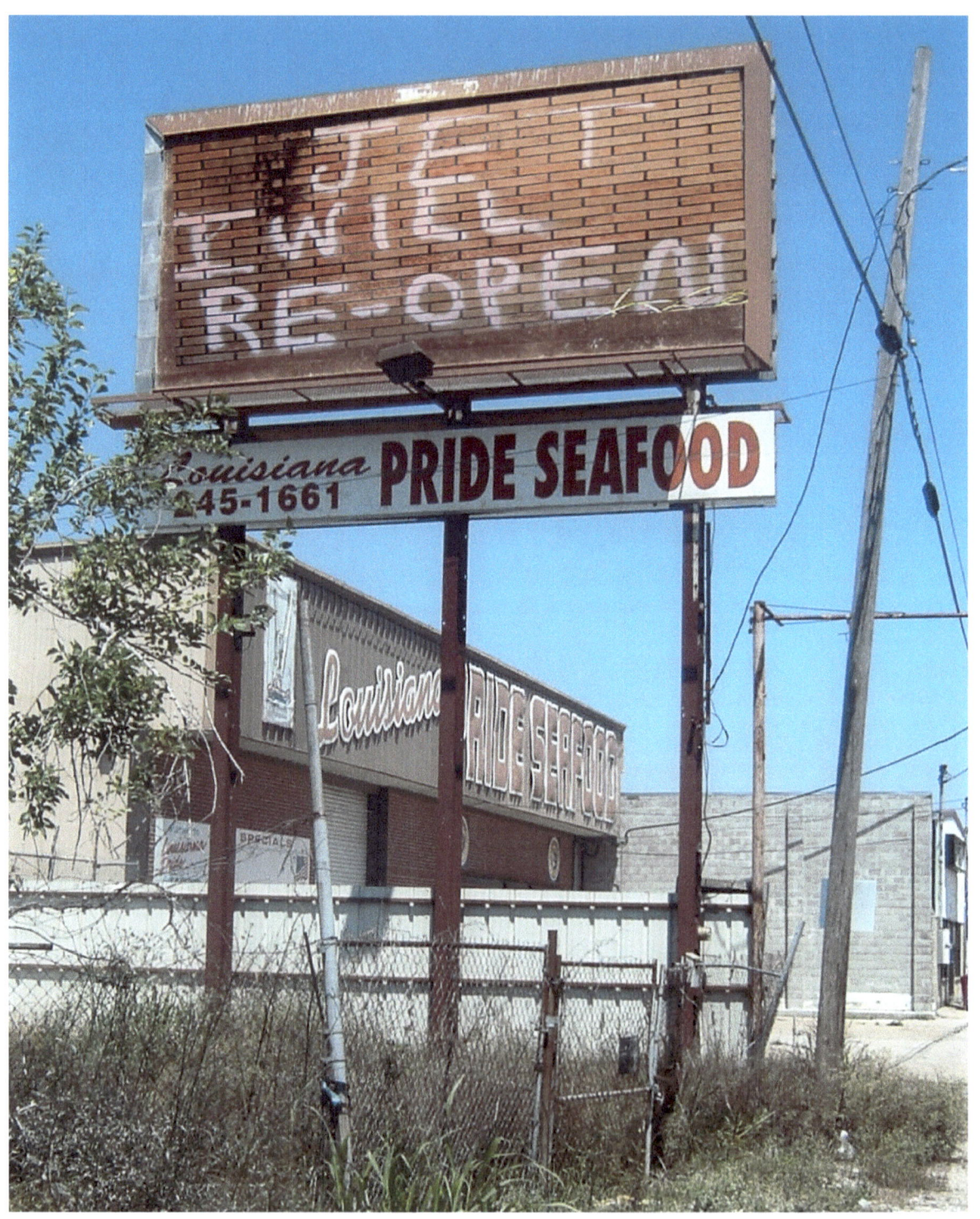

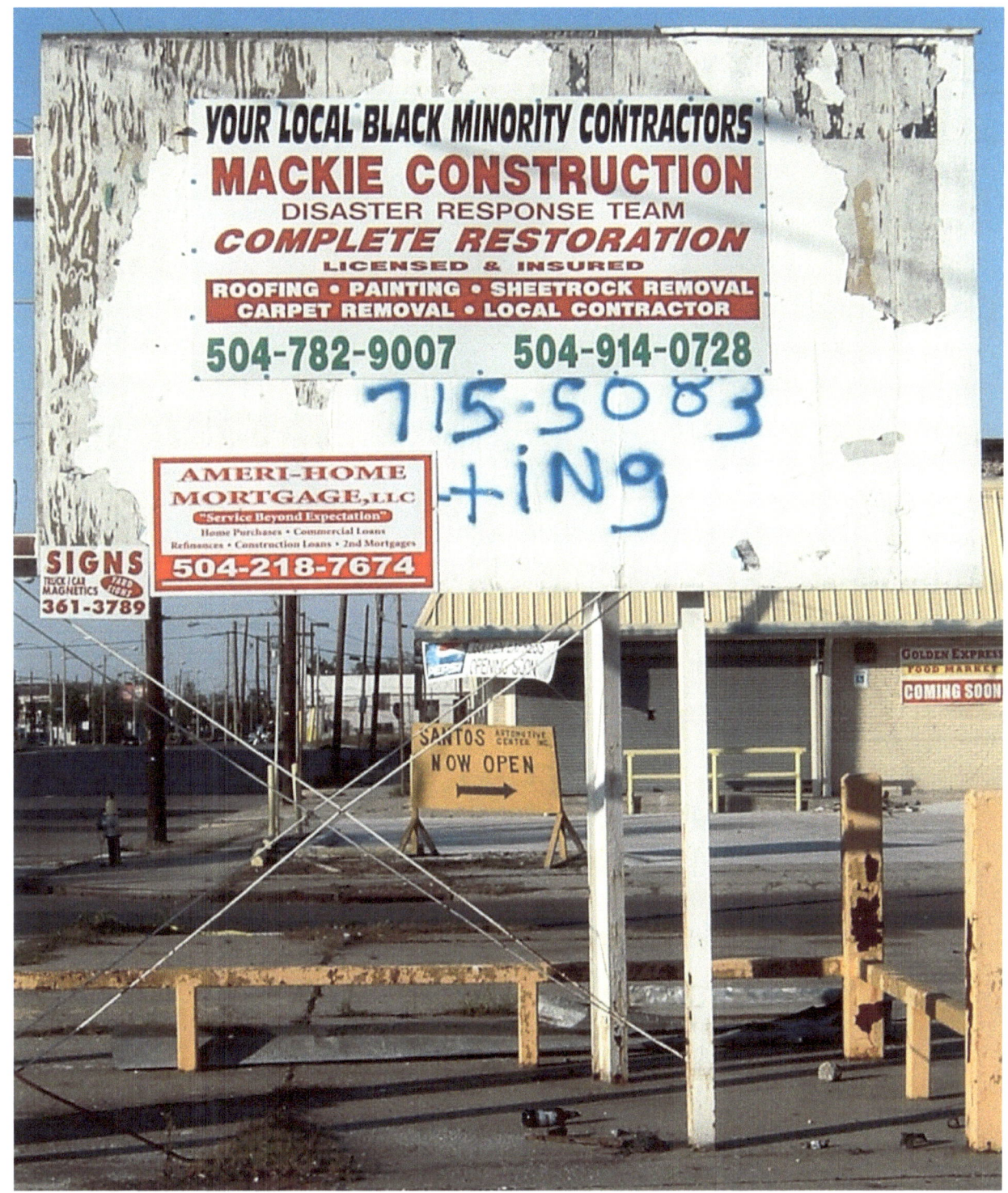

43

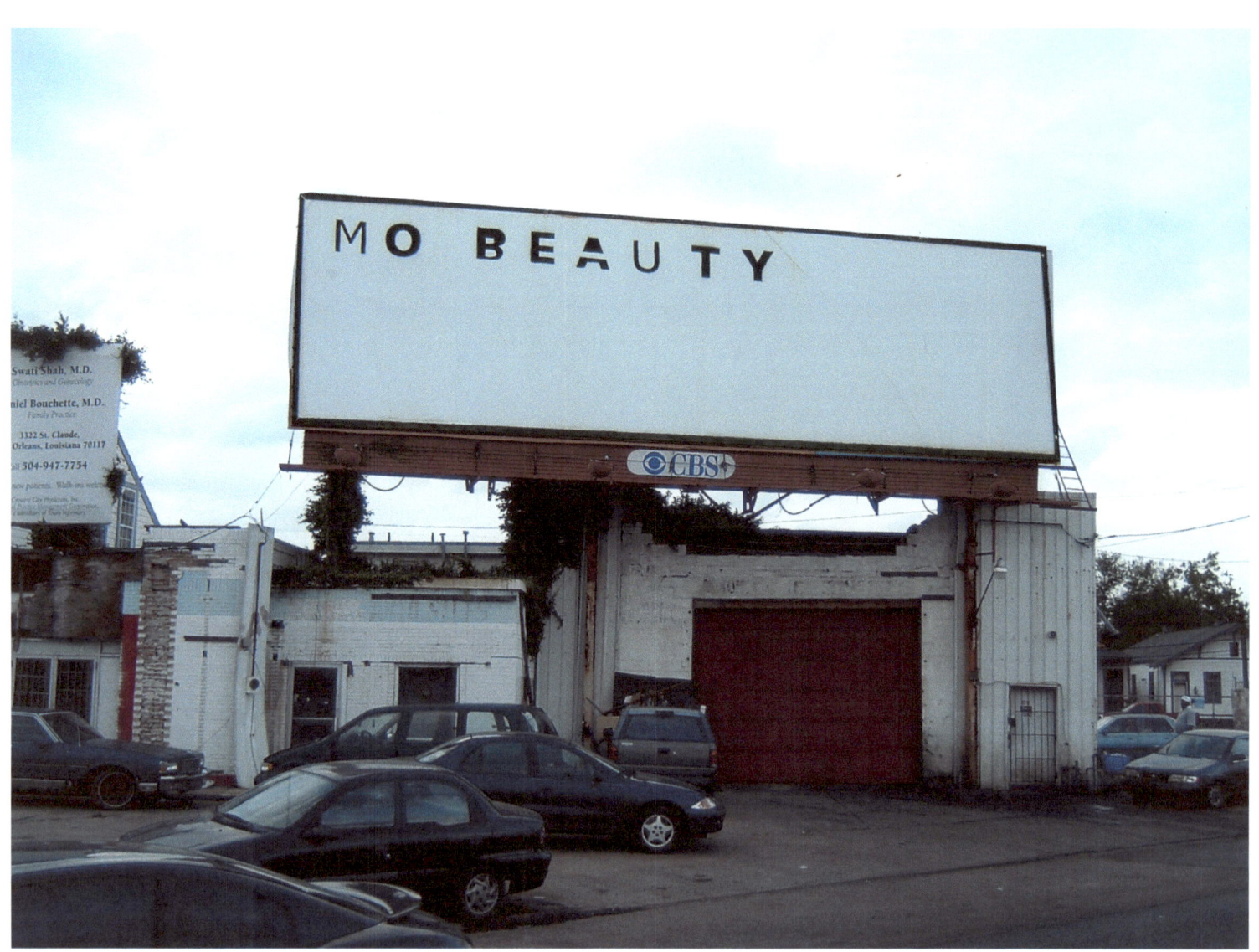

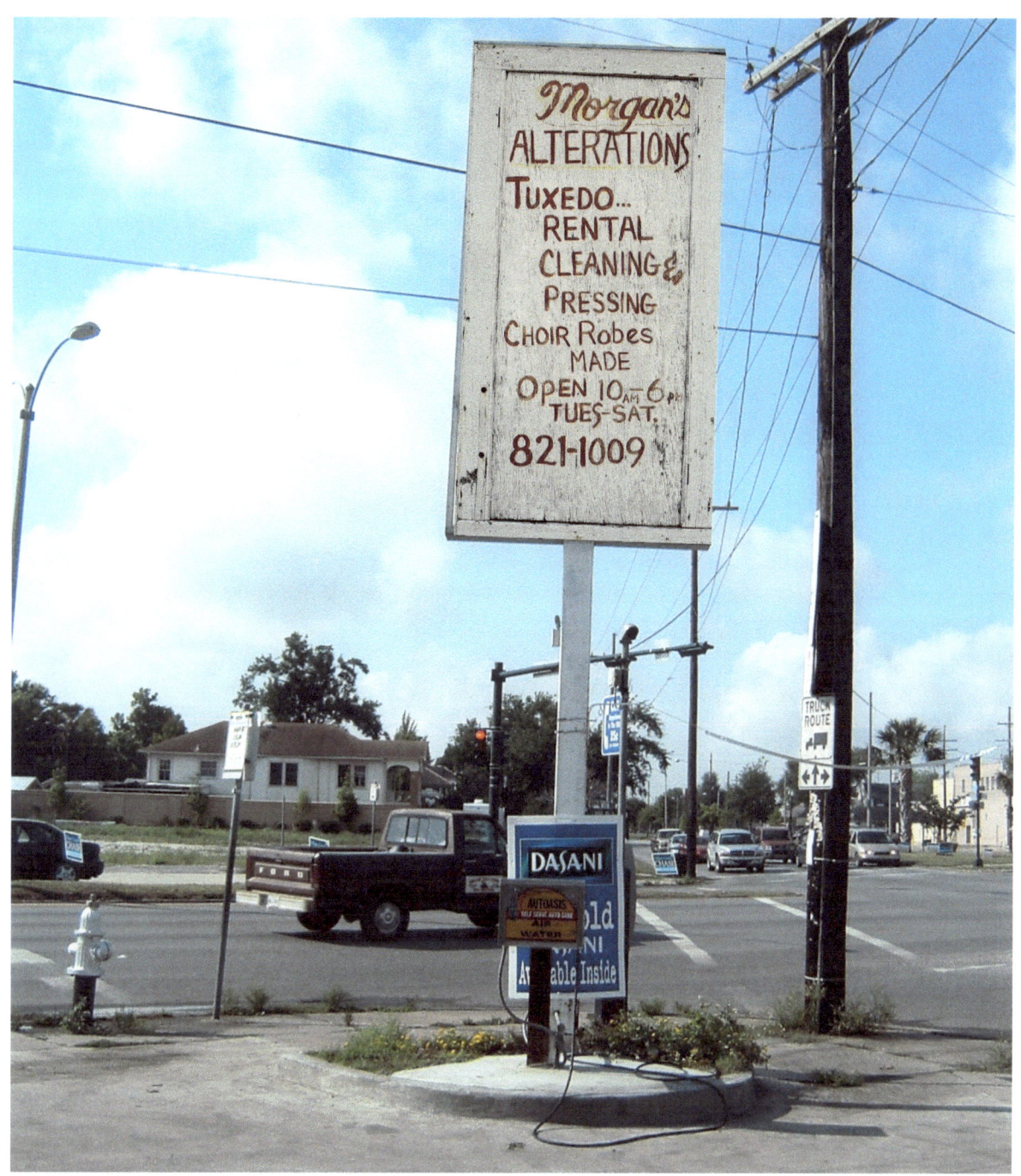

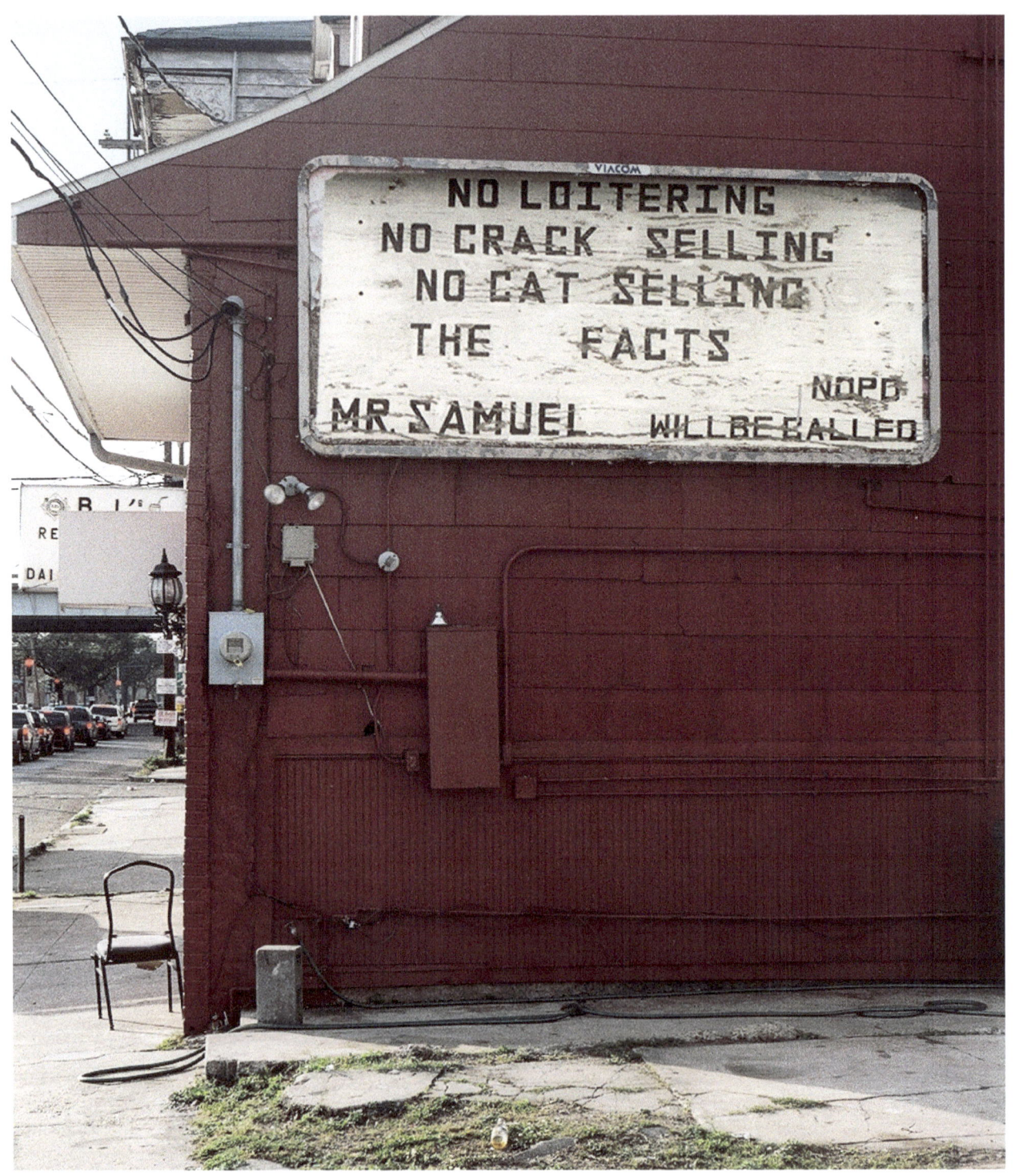

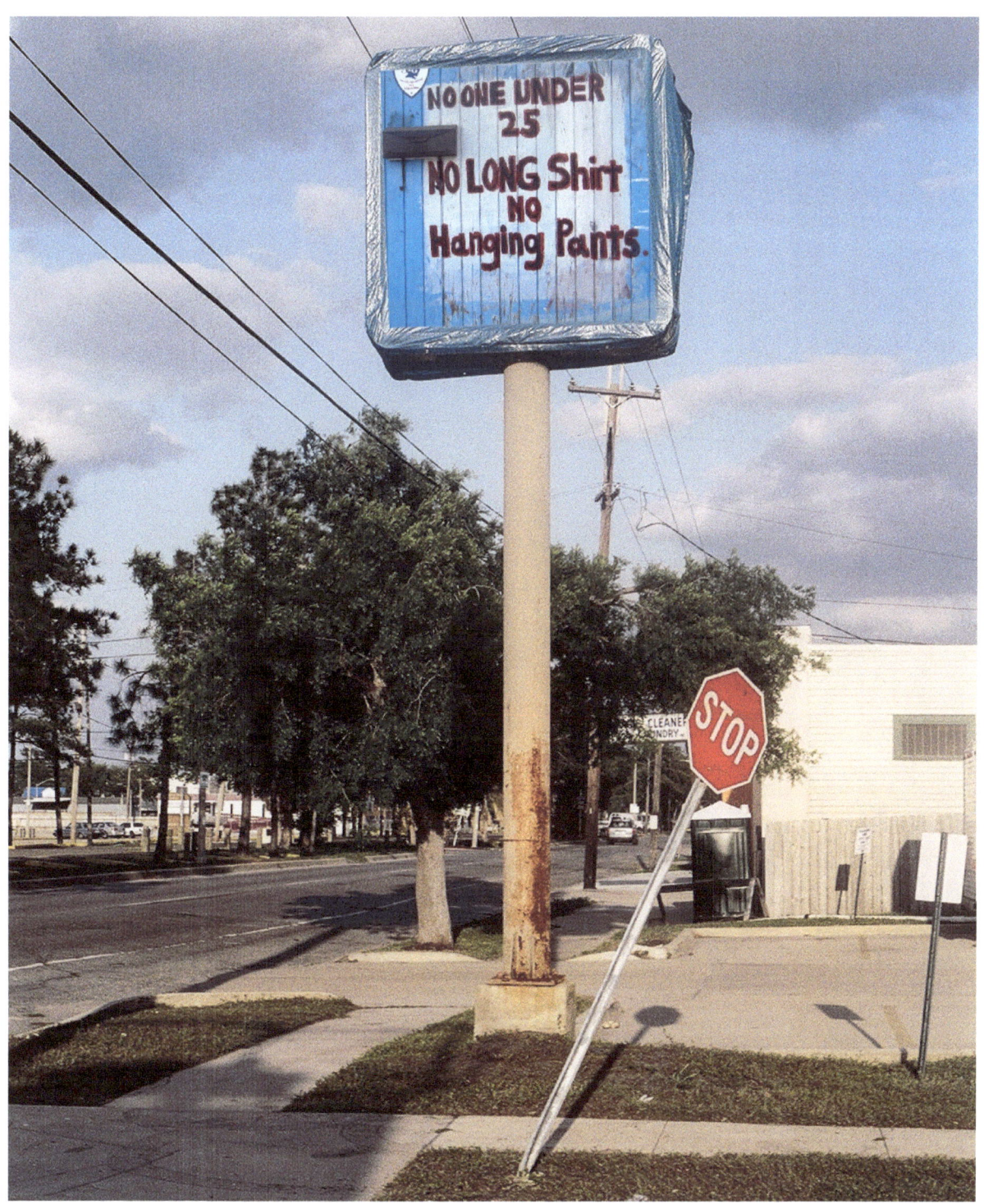

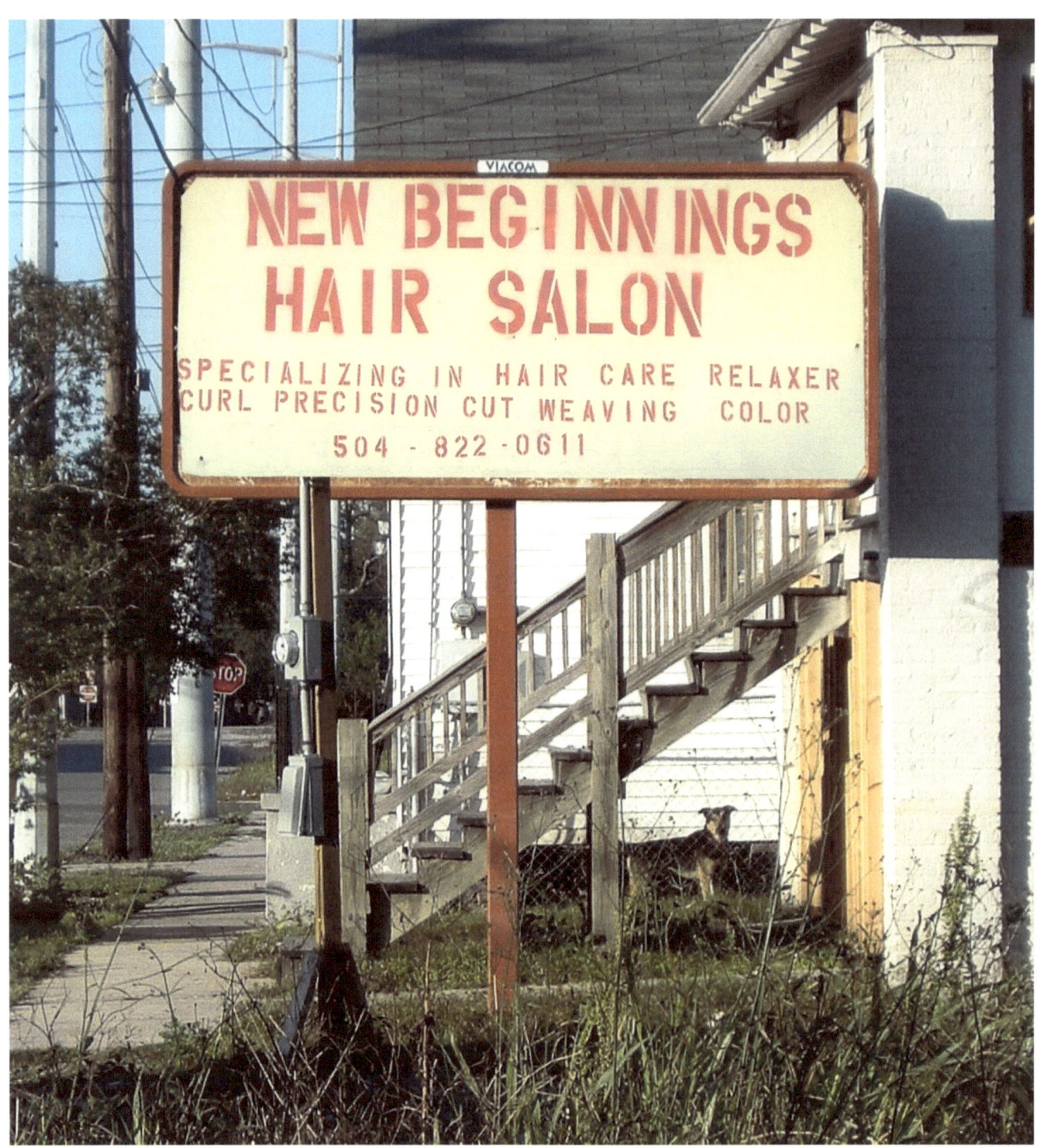

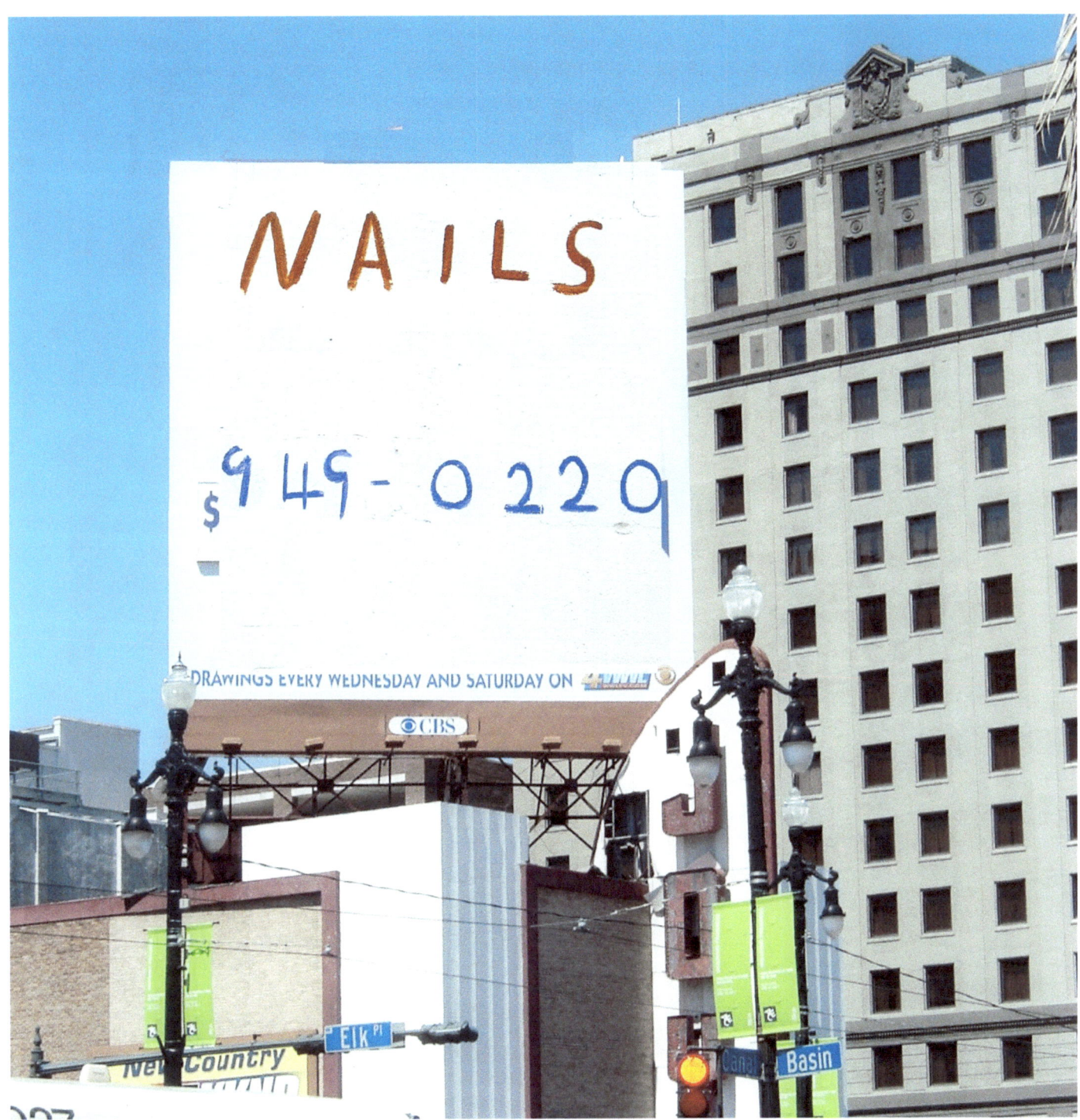

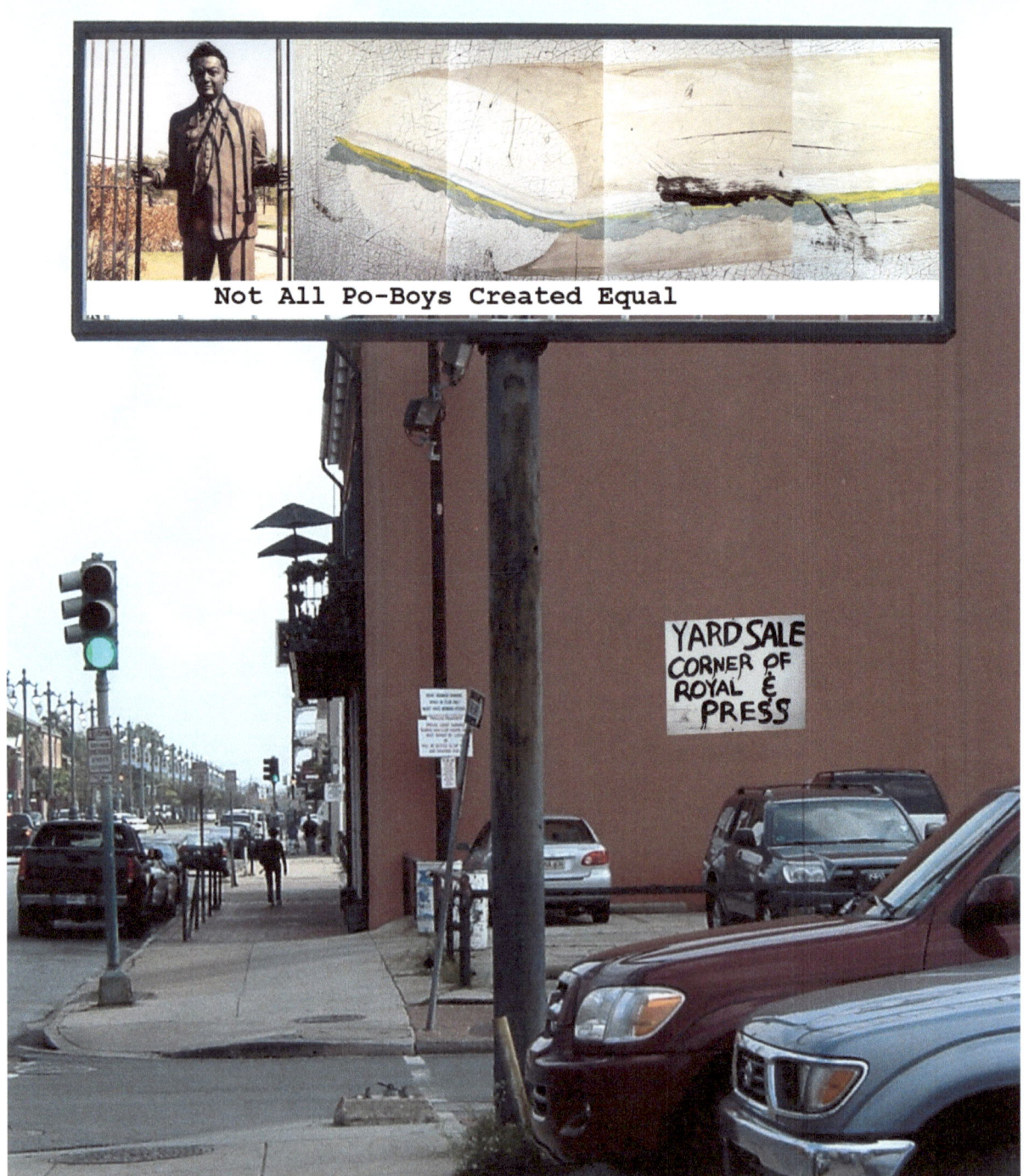

Not All Po-Boys Created Equal

50

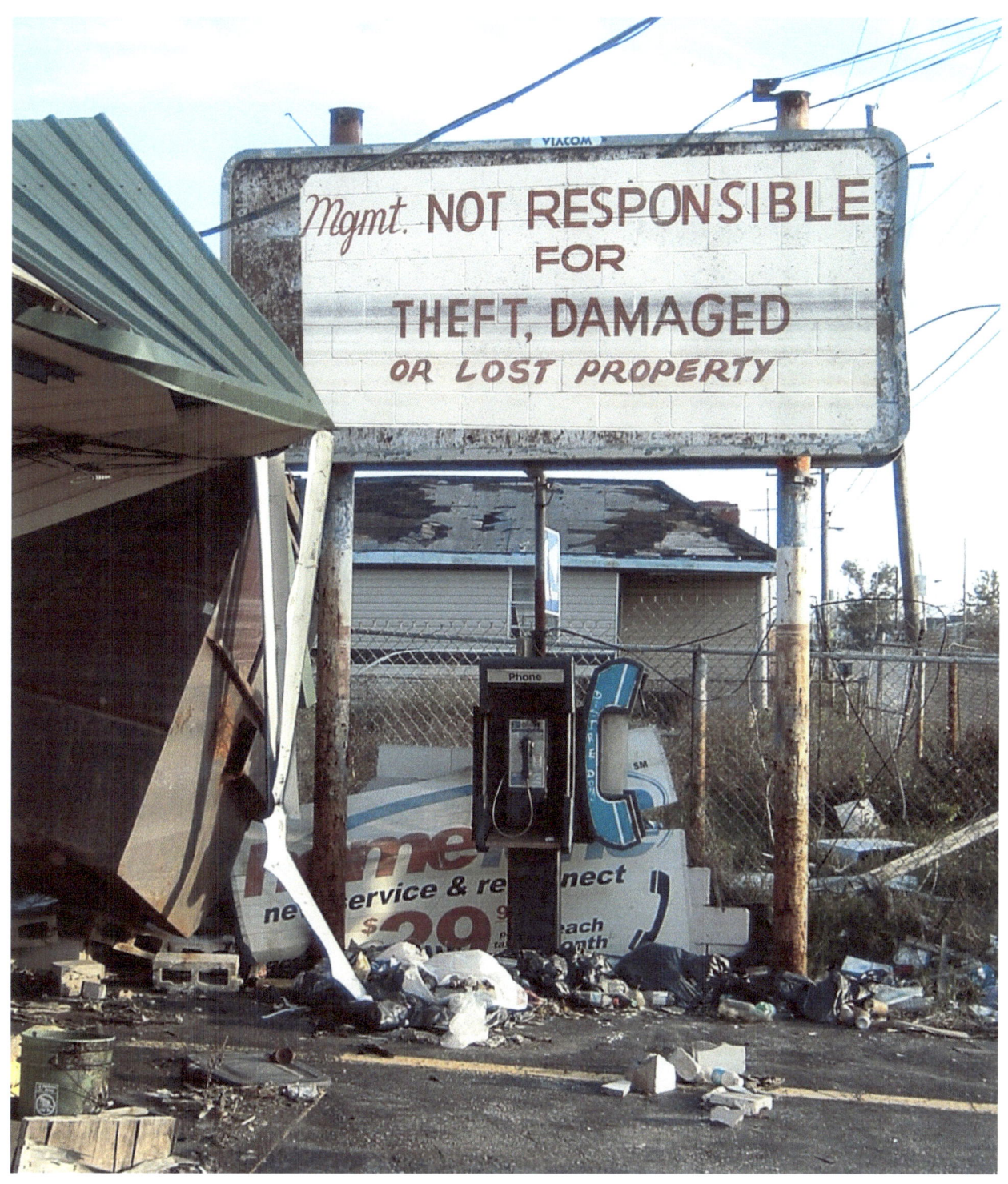

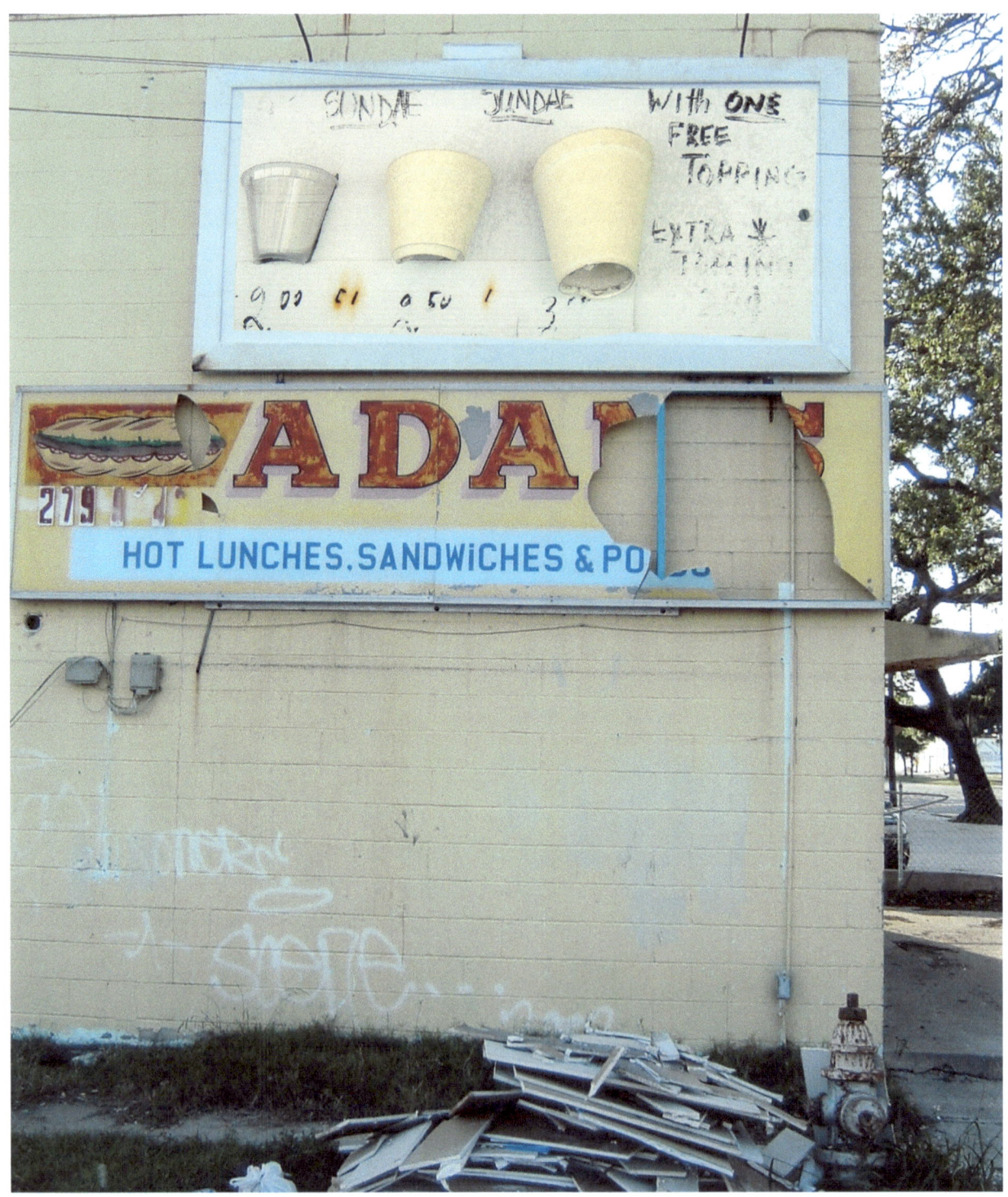

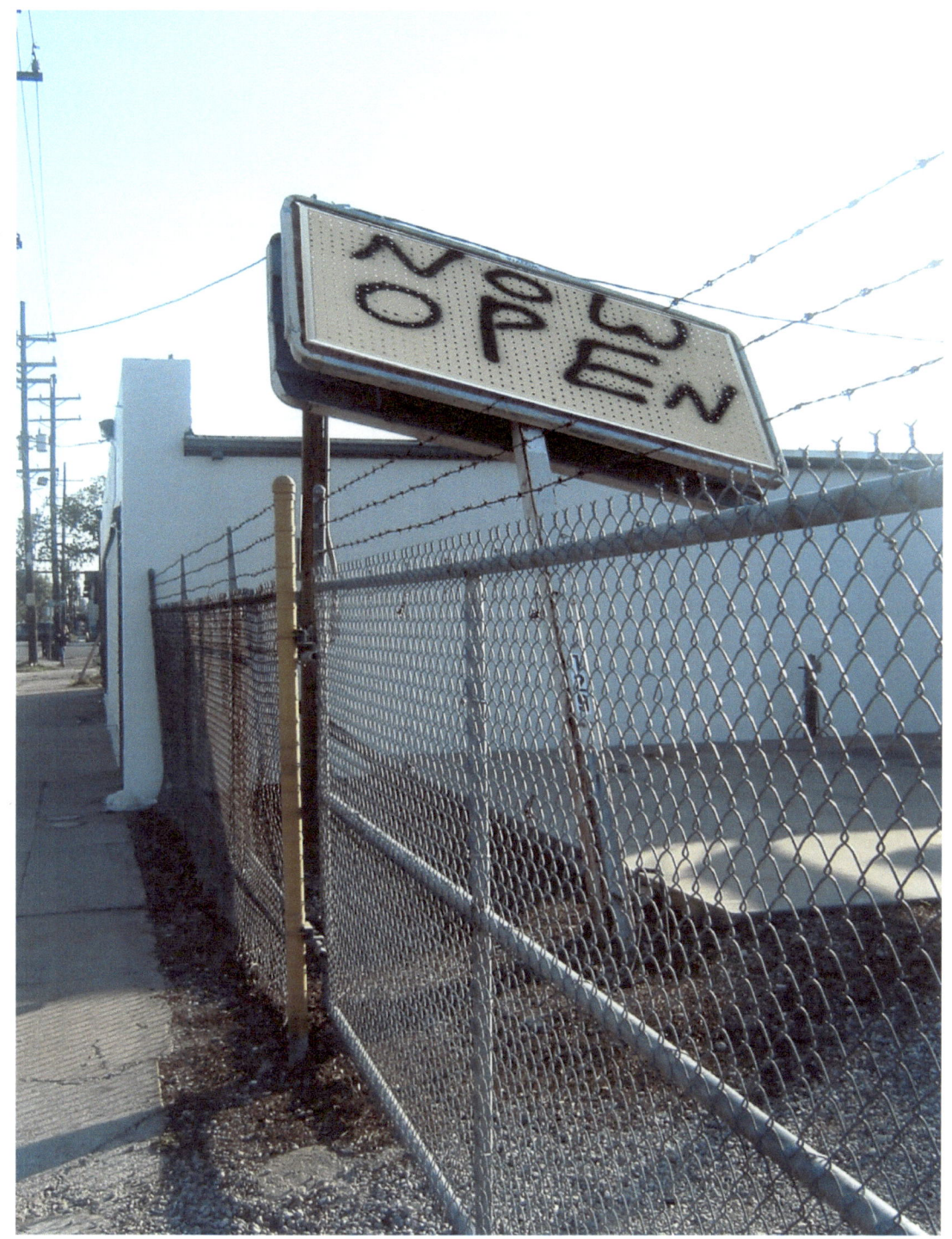

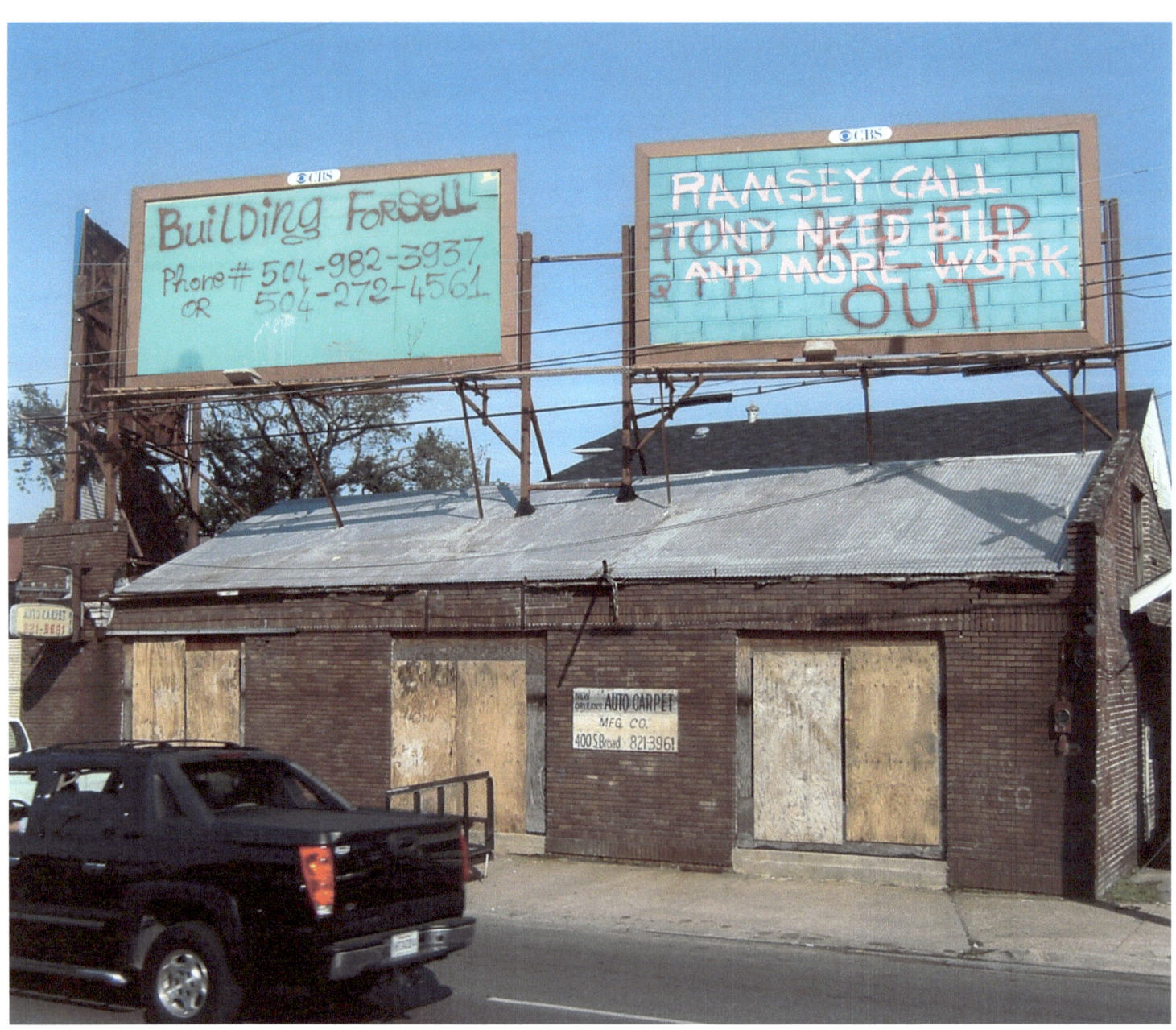

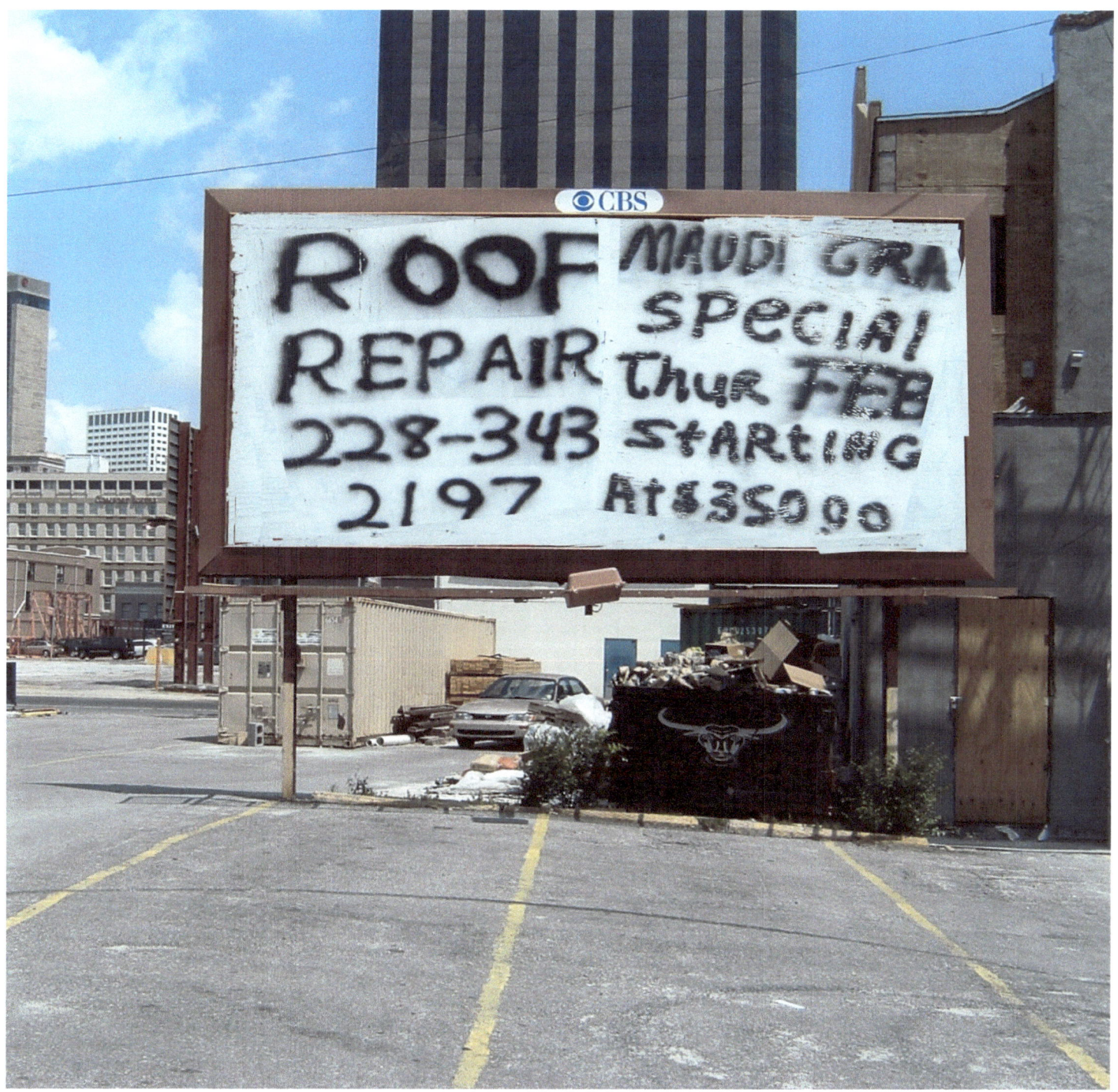

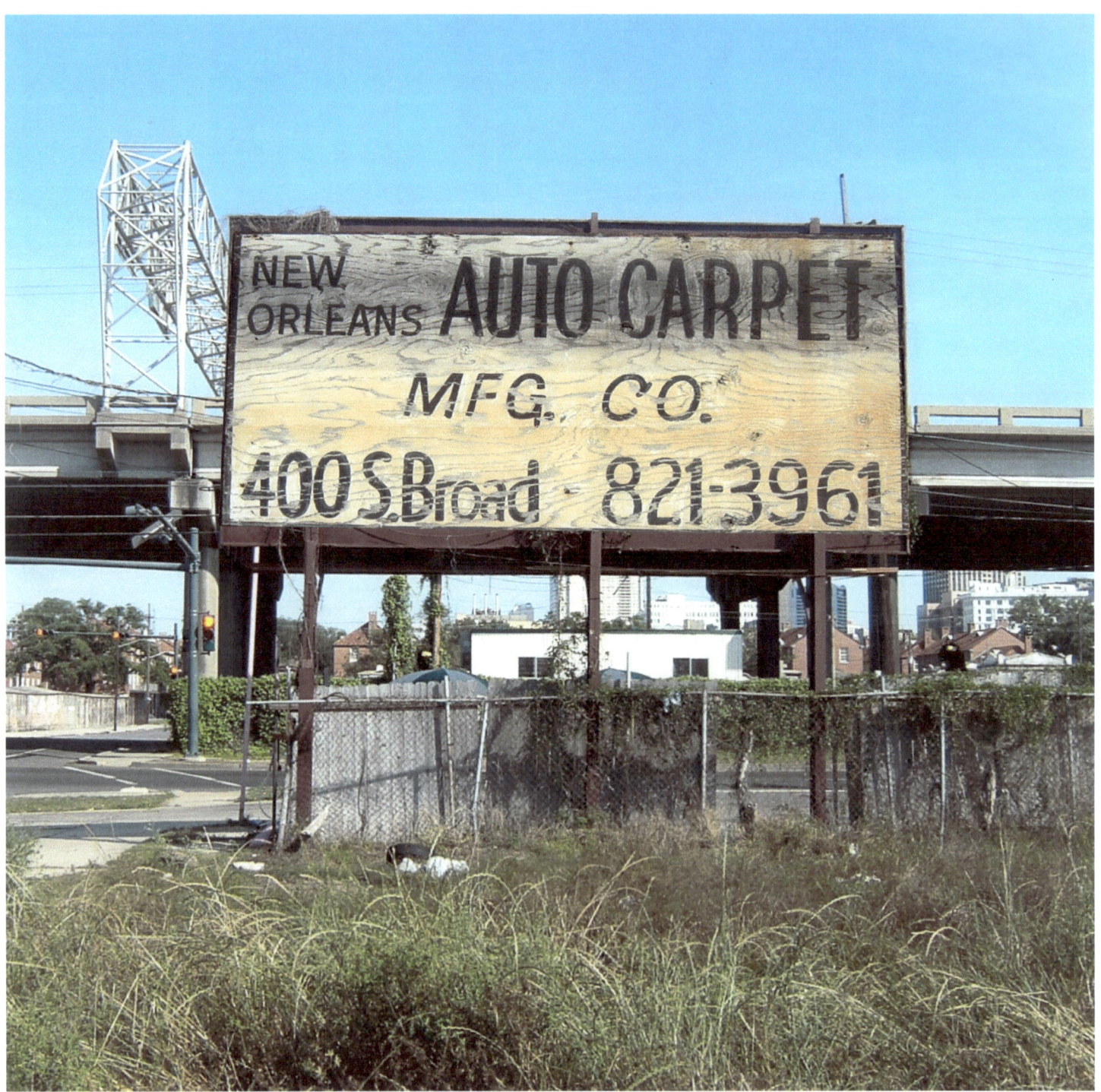

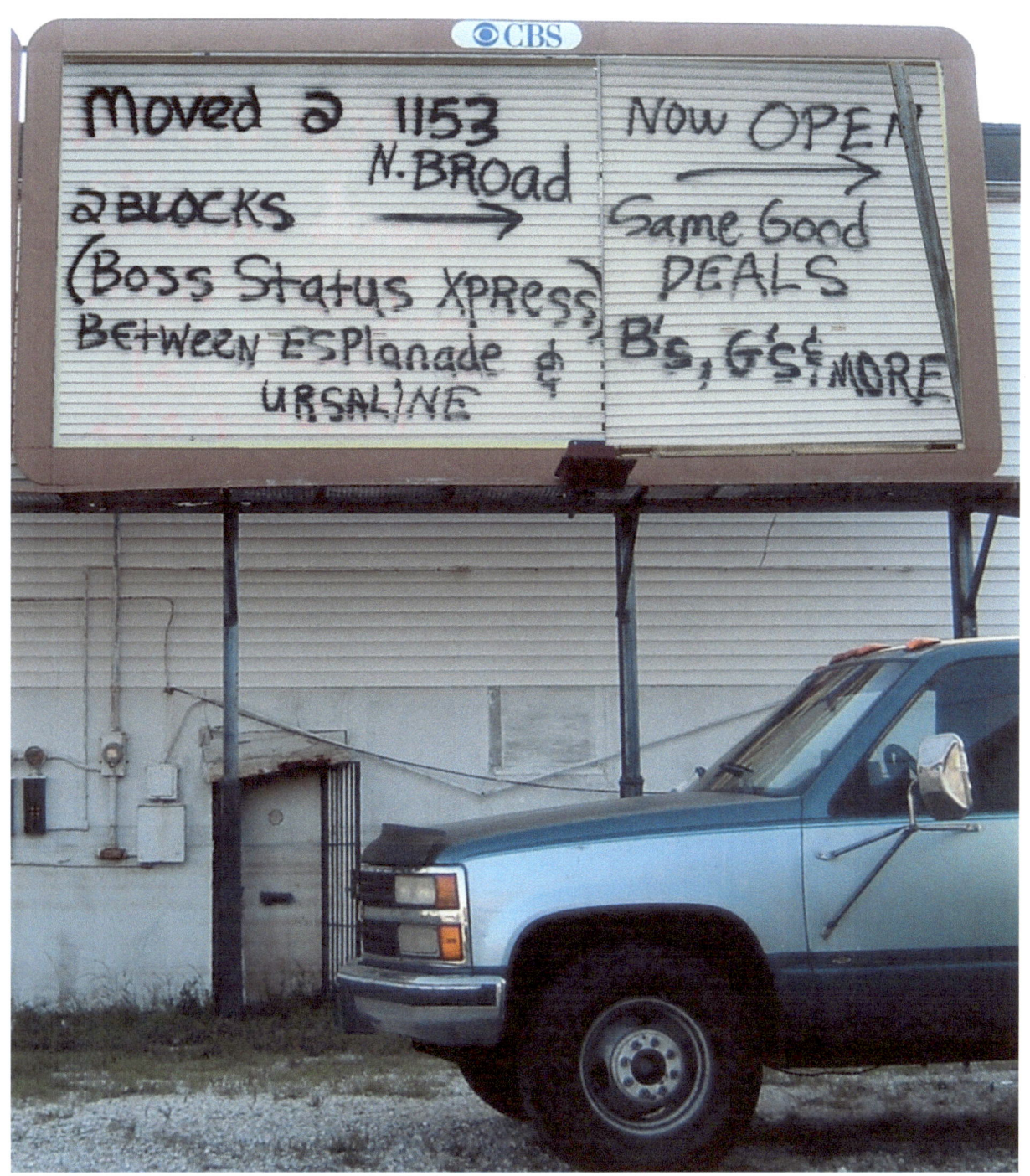

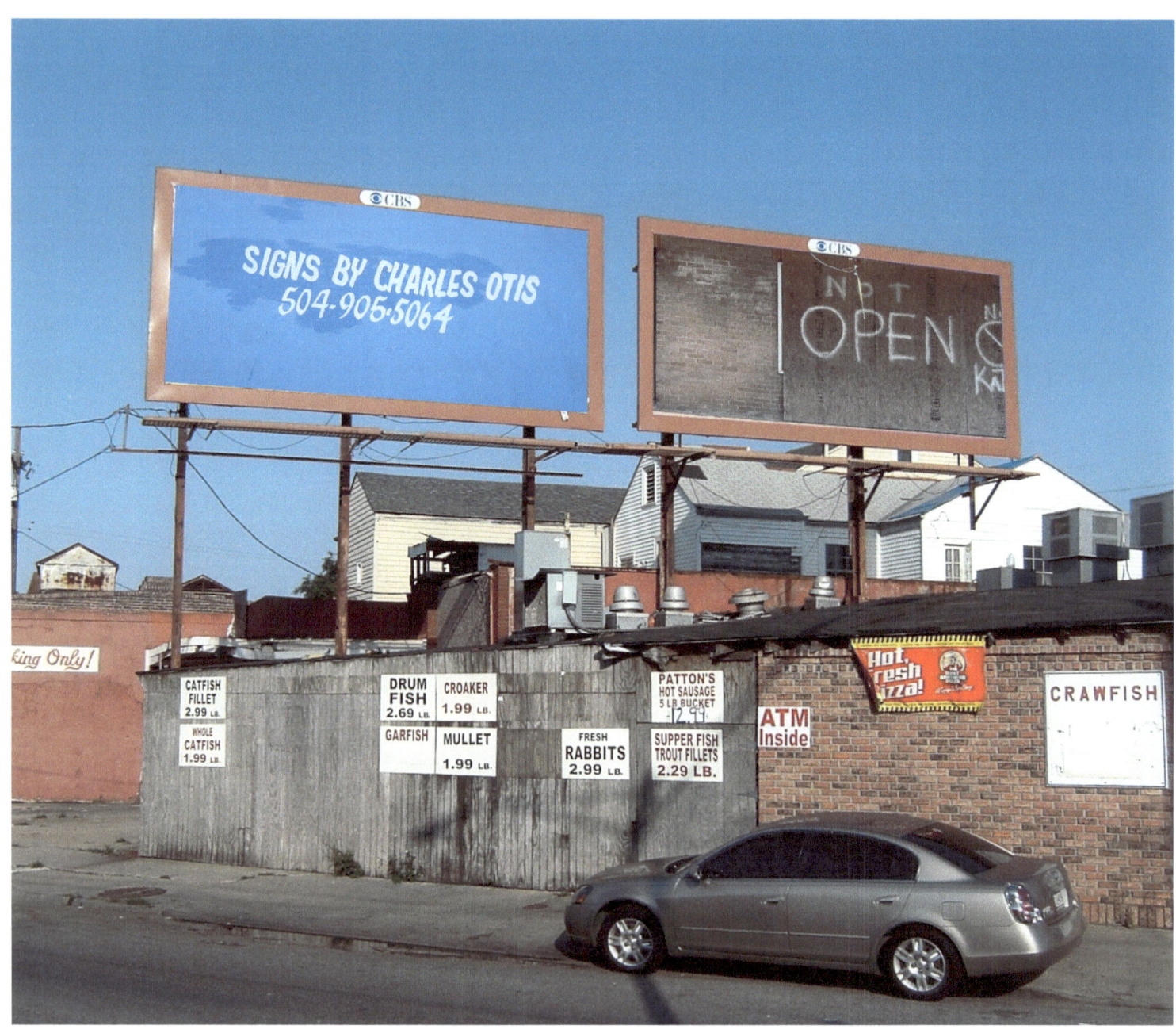

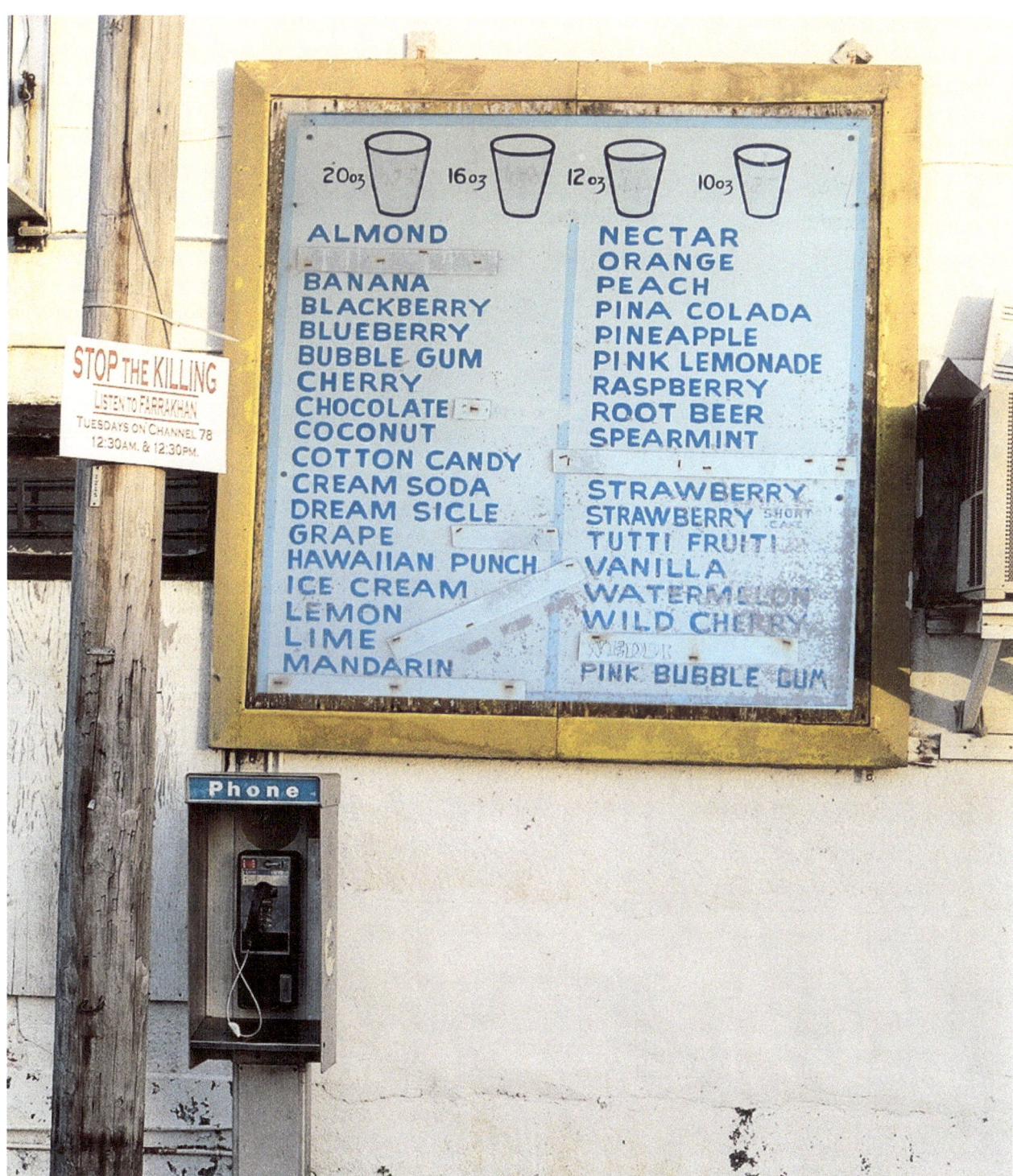

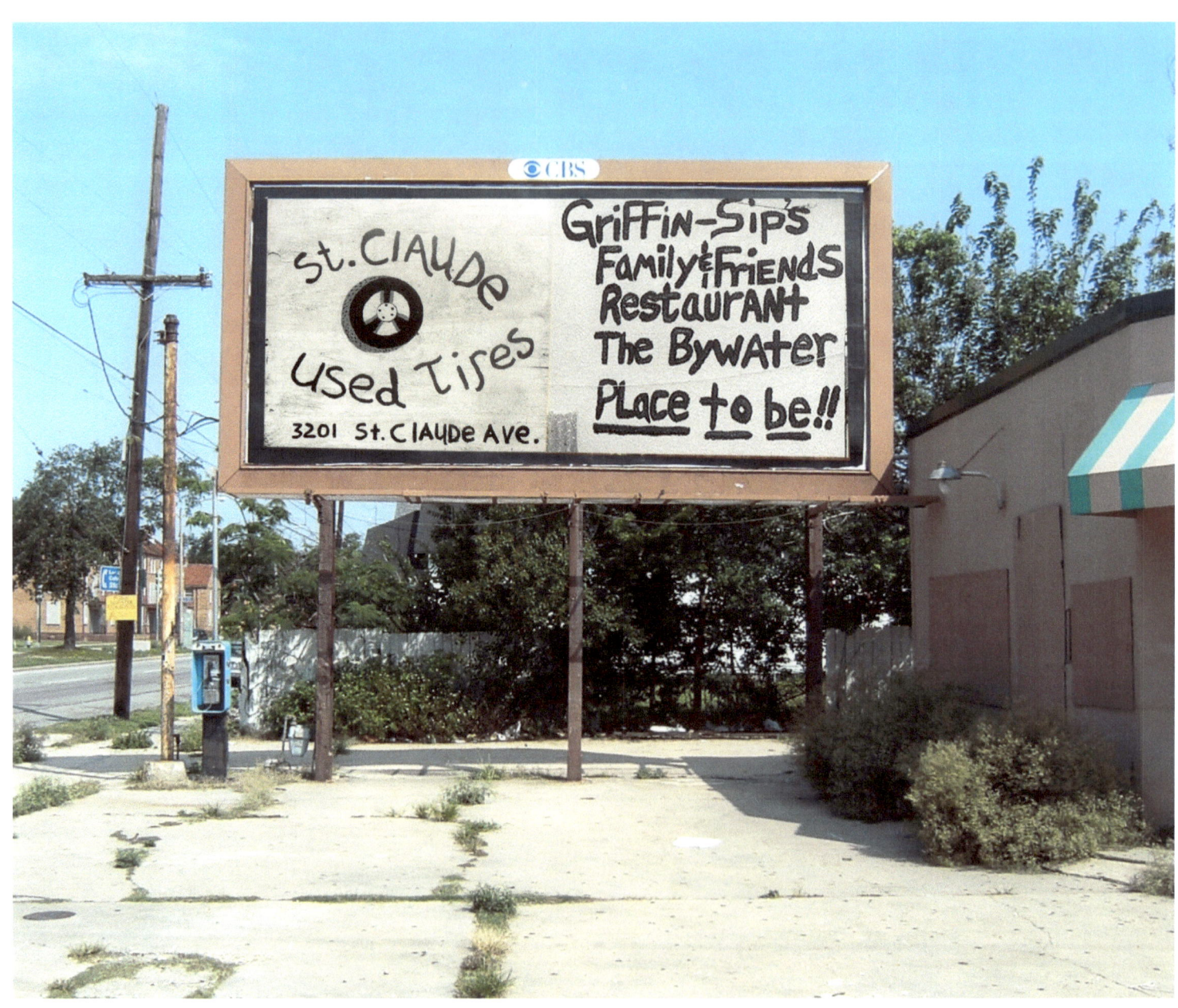

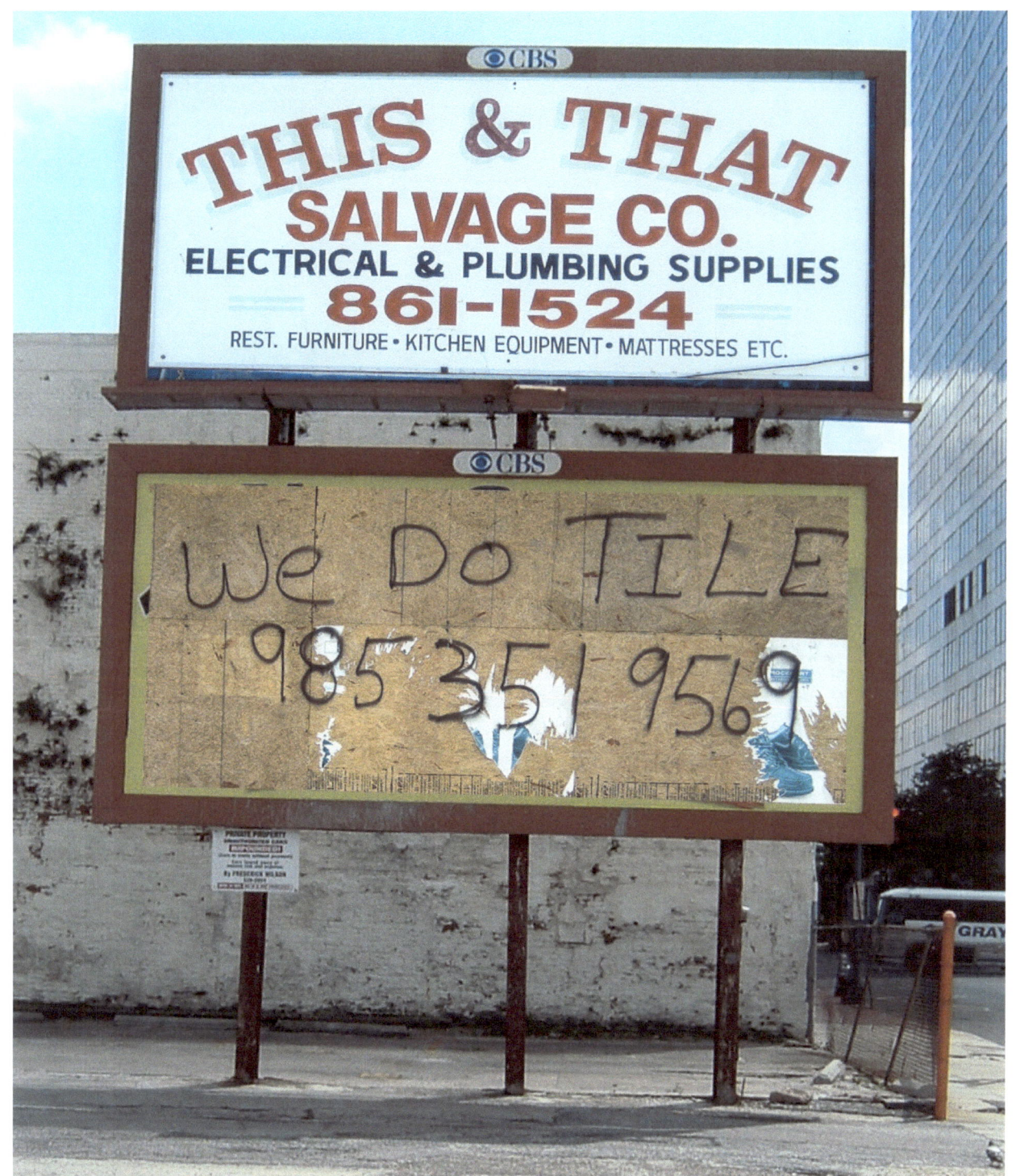

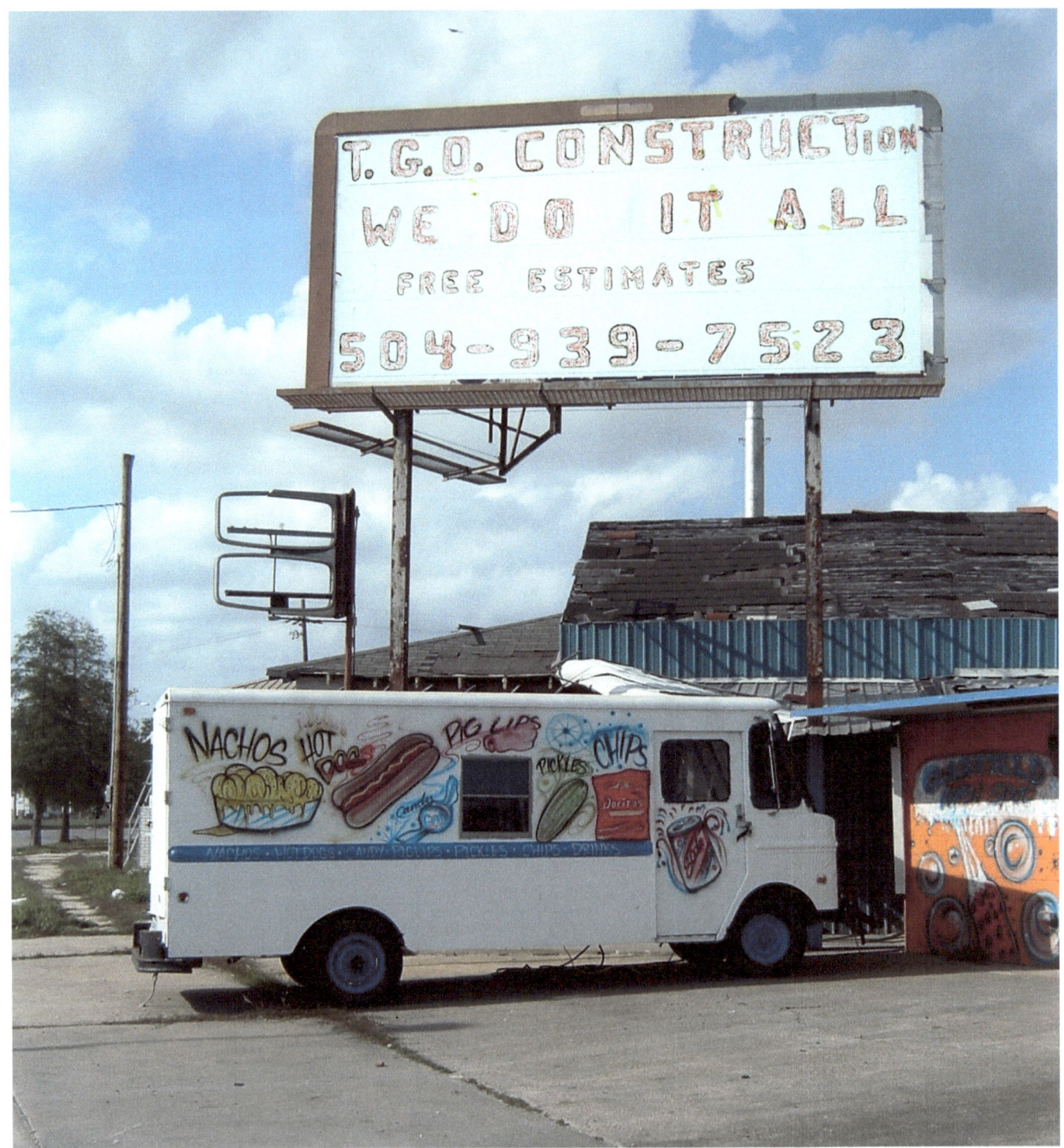

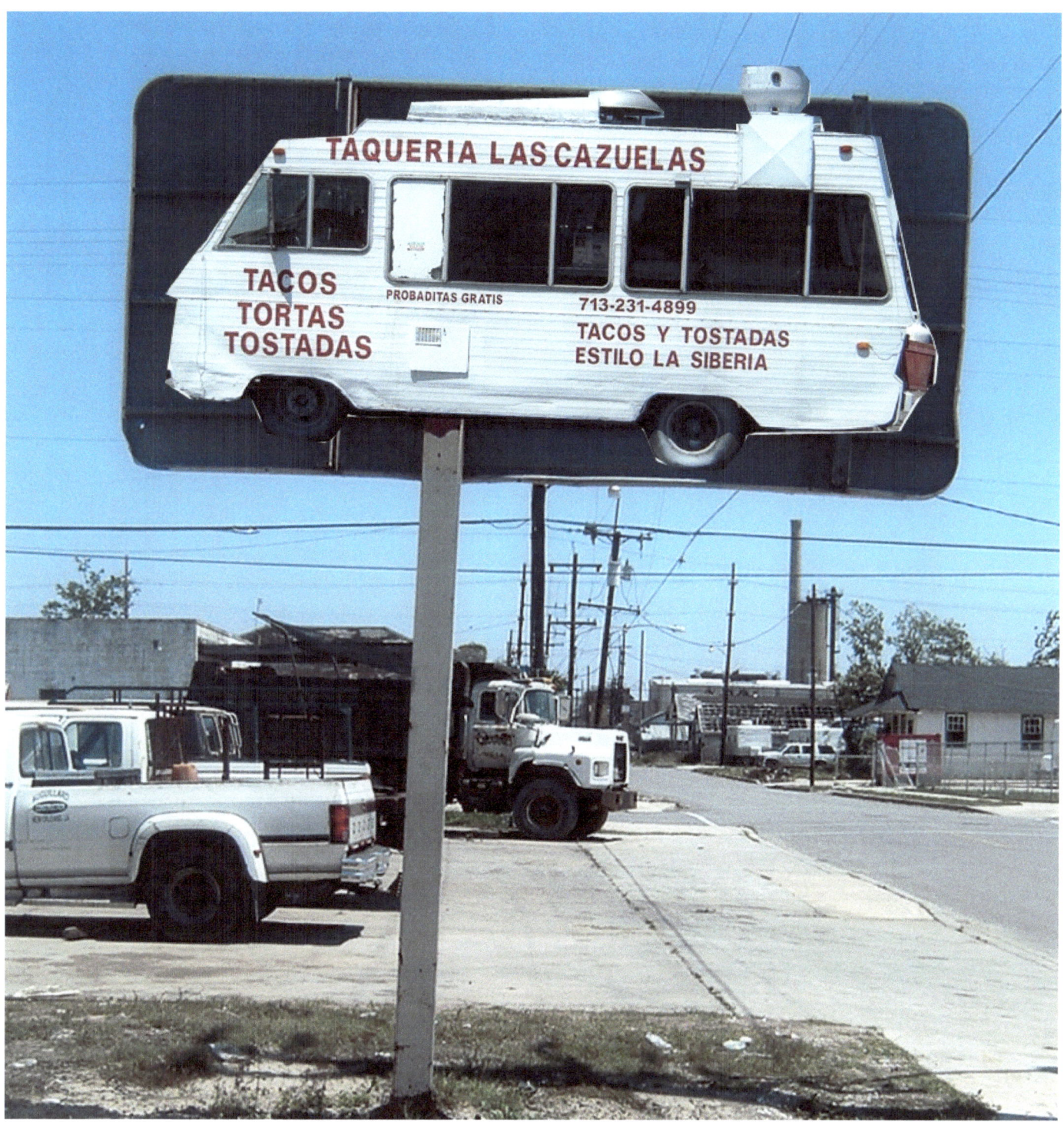

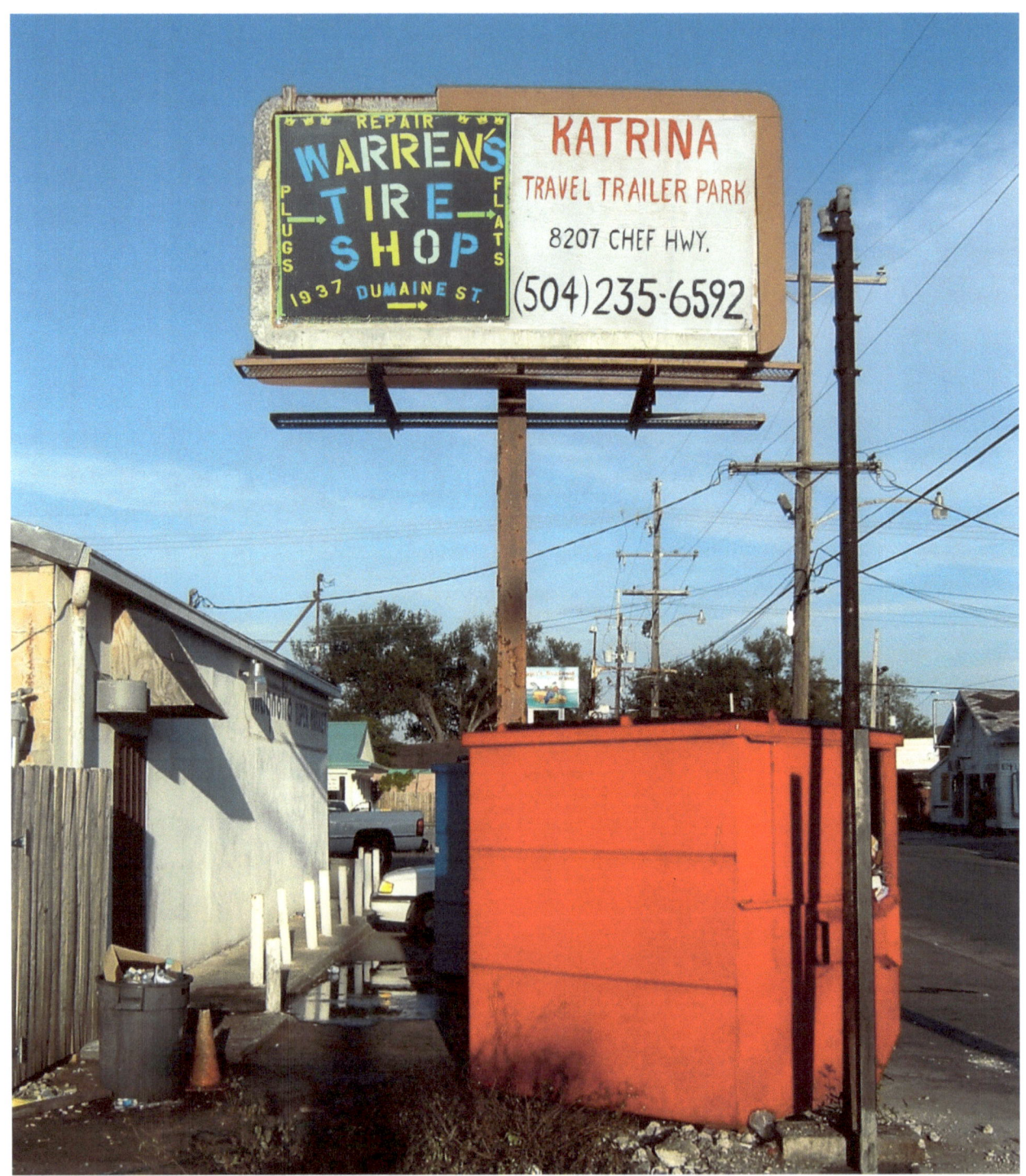

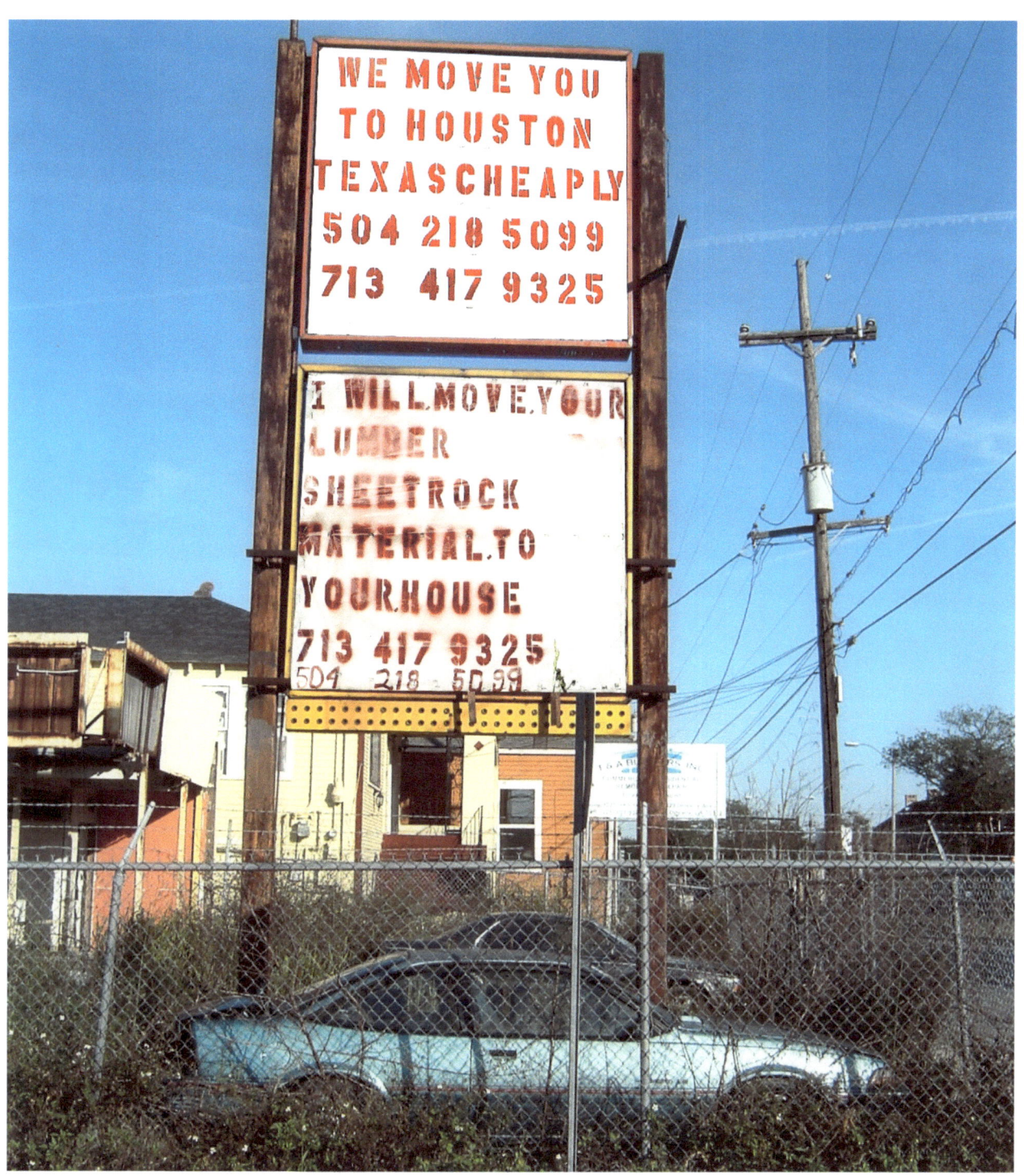

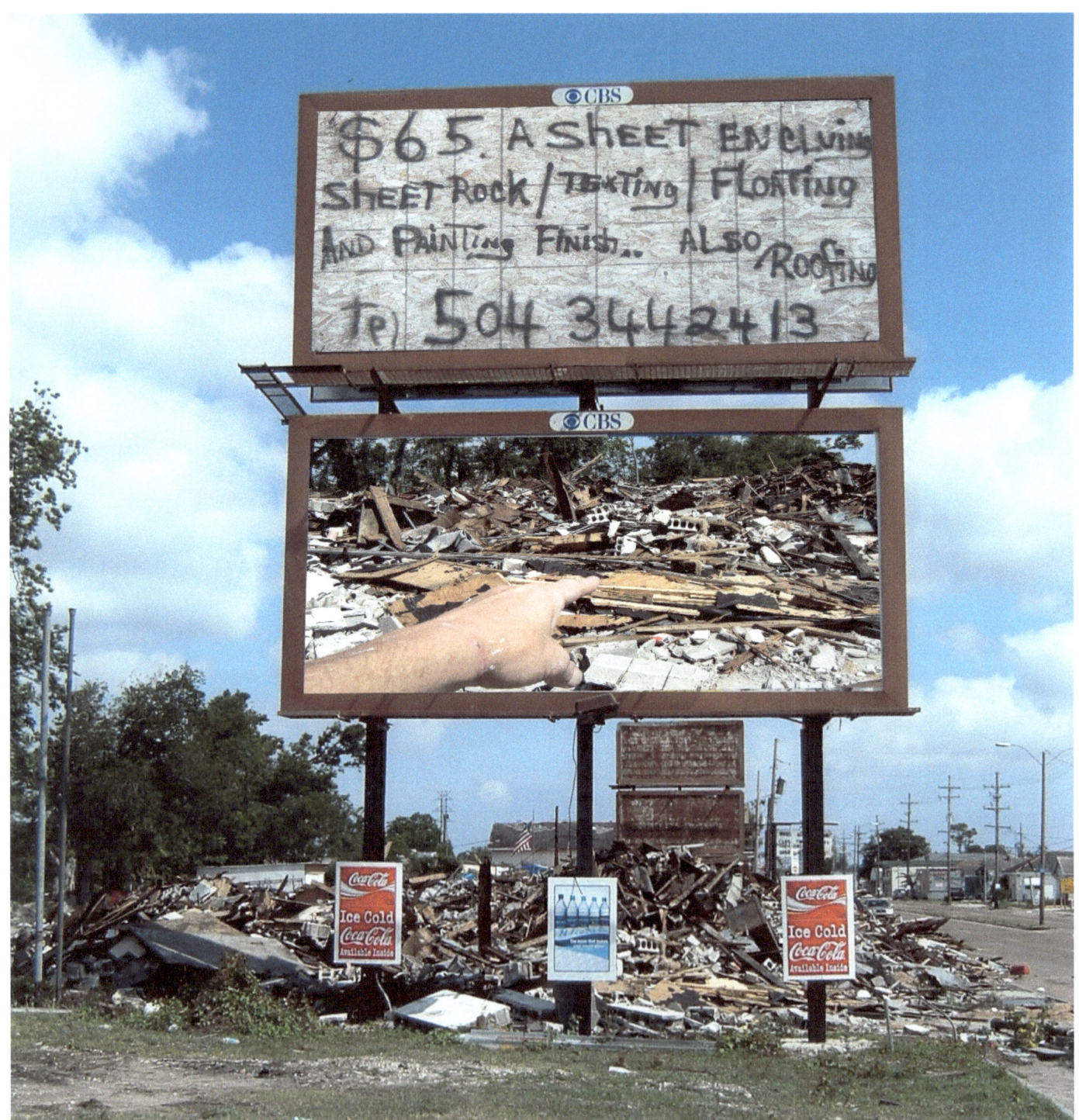

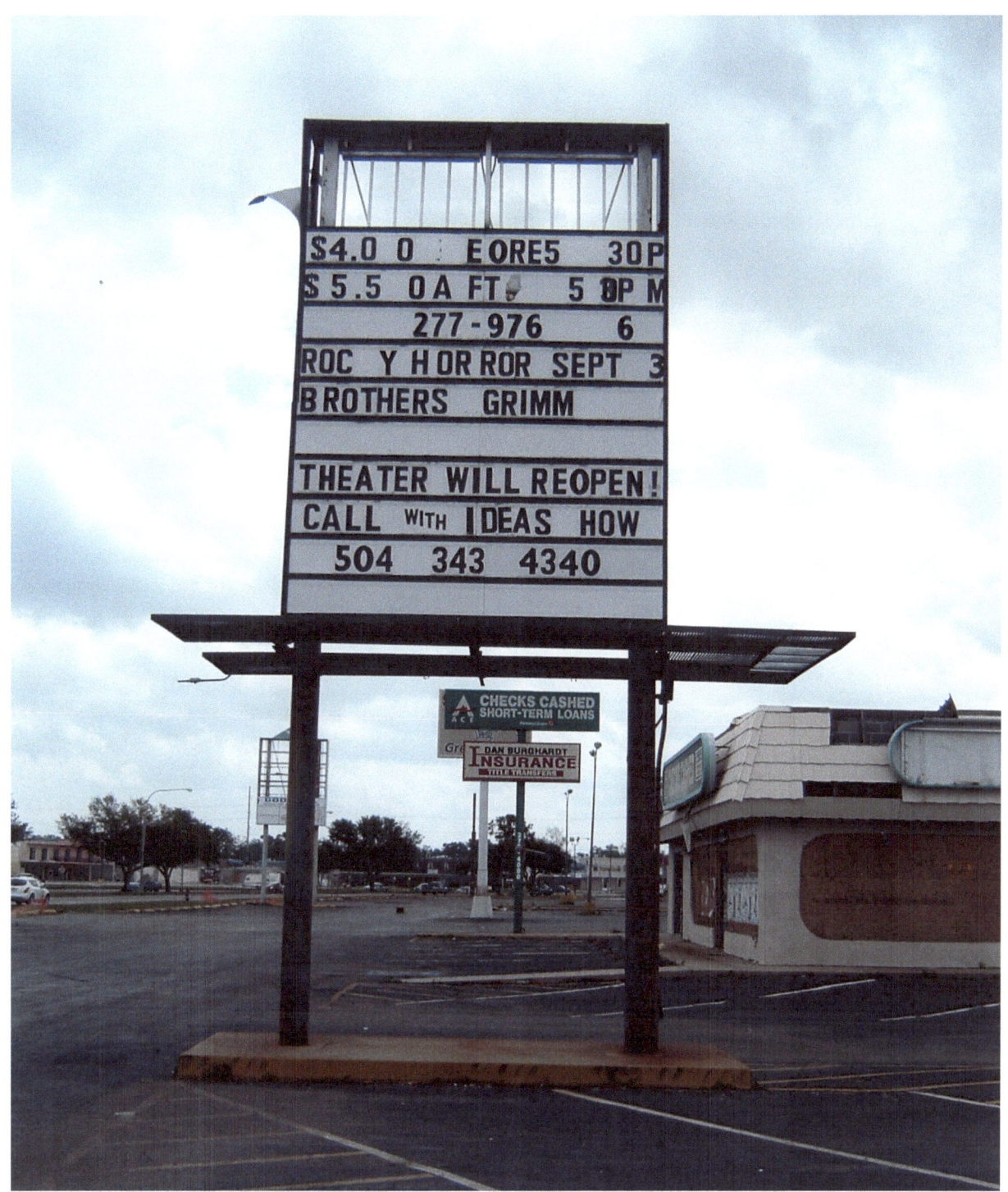

One day collected signs
framed nothing but blue sky
and wires and clouds and dreams of services to supply
EXHIBITION OPPORTUNITY FOR VISUAL ARTISTS IN NEW ORLEANS

THE PARENTS OF DRED WERE AT IT AGAIN

sunny and fine and in the wrong place at the wrong time –

trying to follow Billy's advice – Let Creative Energy – brought me to the

intersection of Orleans x AnY Food Mart.

This is not *any* Food Mart. The *N* is a poor man's ampersand.

I stopped to camera collect it for a private New Orleans I was making,

where Justice may not reign, but Underperforming Billboards Dream.

Services on painted plywood, wire-tied eye level to a telephone pole by

the stop sign, are promoted (digitally) to rub shoulders with SUVs,

Hospitals, Bottled Spirits, Hamburgers to announce, for example,

Cheap Stumps Removal 537-2187

and I thought the AnY Food Store deserved as much.

Near some vacated public housing projects though well built and historic,

had received 1/4 inch of water after the levees broke so residents were

evicted permanently to demolish the housing and redevelop the property

–these buildings were hard to police.   Now one has time to stop his

cruiser and pounce on my Corolla, where I sit fiddling with settings on a

digital camera.

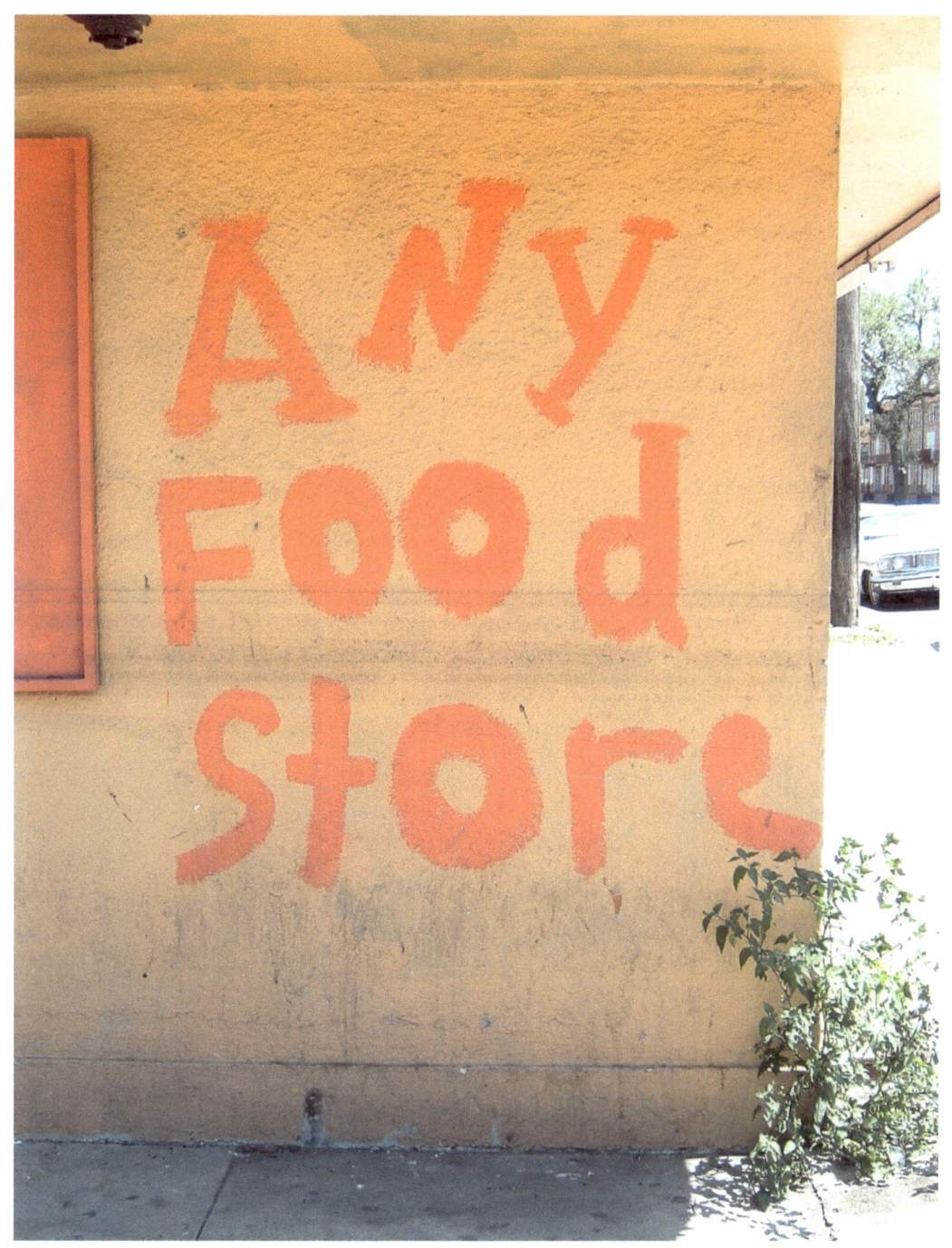

In this hood I could:

a) be buying drugs

b) be admiring a hand painted *n* as ampersand

c) my problem is in the explaining

d) in my pocket, a Louisiana Safety Net

Matchbook yellow cover black letters

1-800-NOT-GUILTY

A Hubigs Pie Wrapper in the corner of my windshield in lieu of an

inspection tag –I'd have to replace the windshield to get that sticker.

Why do I waste the genius of my $800 Corolla, for surely it is capable of

delivering me to some moist, salt laden everyday Pacific air.

I have persisted in using it to stay here.

The Peace Officer says

- Put your hands on the dashboard where I can see them.

Deep breath.

I collect CS's - is Cuffed & Searched Coming Soon?

My Language Photography was going to blow the lid off of this place

and we can't have that.

I lift my hands.

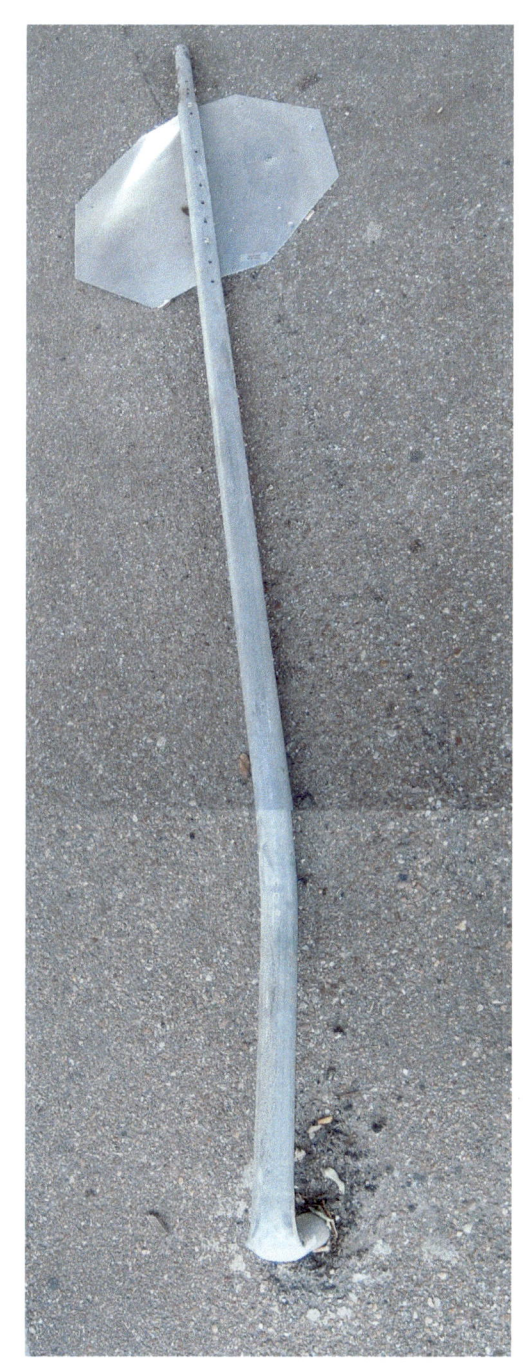

Appendix:

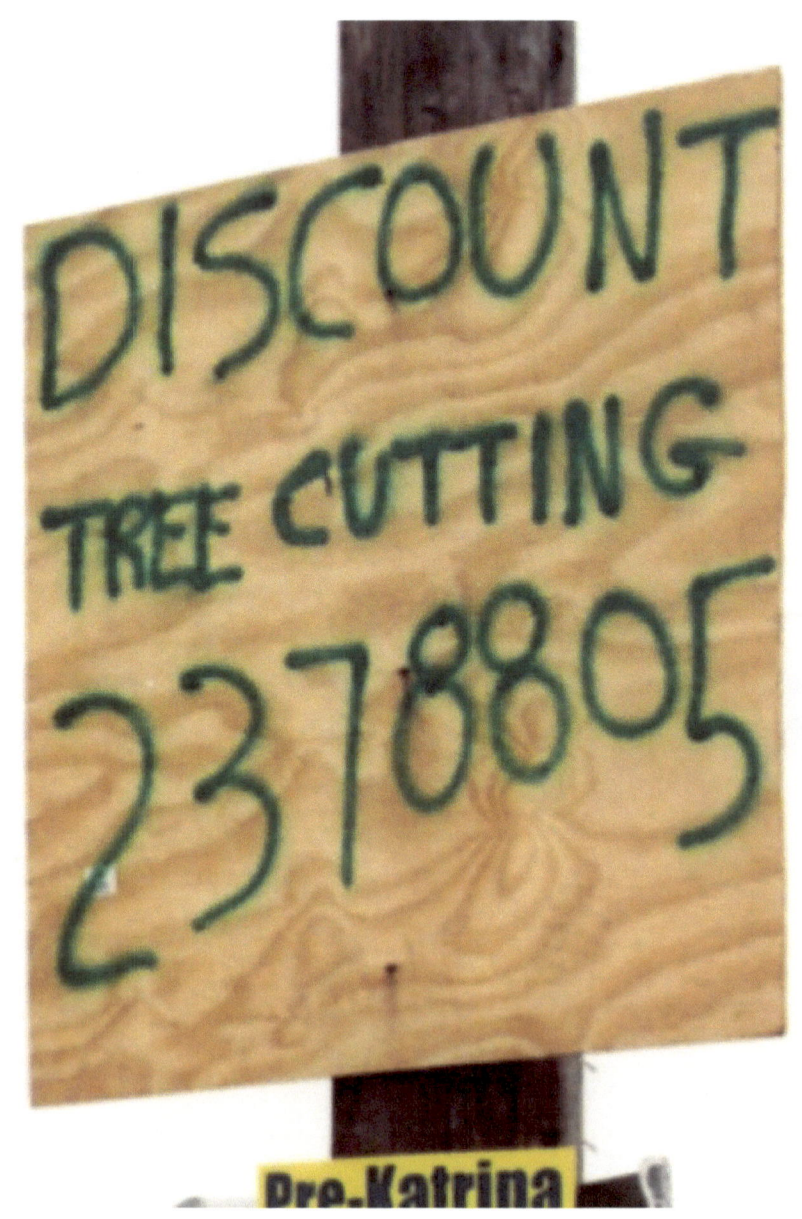

Most of these pictures were taken in 2005-8. In the beginning the signs were made on unprimed plywood. Then pressboard, primed white, and some time after came the orange border. A few years ago, the phone number changed. Lately a pair of sticks are tacked horizontally to reinforce the sign to make it more durable. Had I kept up with every placement I've seen, this folio would exceed 100 pages, and I sigh with admiration every time I see one without camera. To my eye it conveys all you want in a tree trimmer: competitive rates, consistency, height, audacity, cunning and persistence.   Now I'm back on the beat, trying to keep up with the latest, aspiring to collect them all and publish the definitive edition of **DISCOUNT TREE CUTTING.**

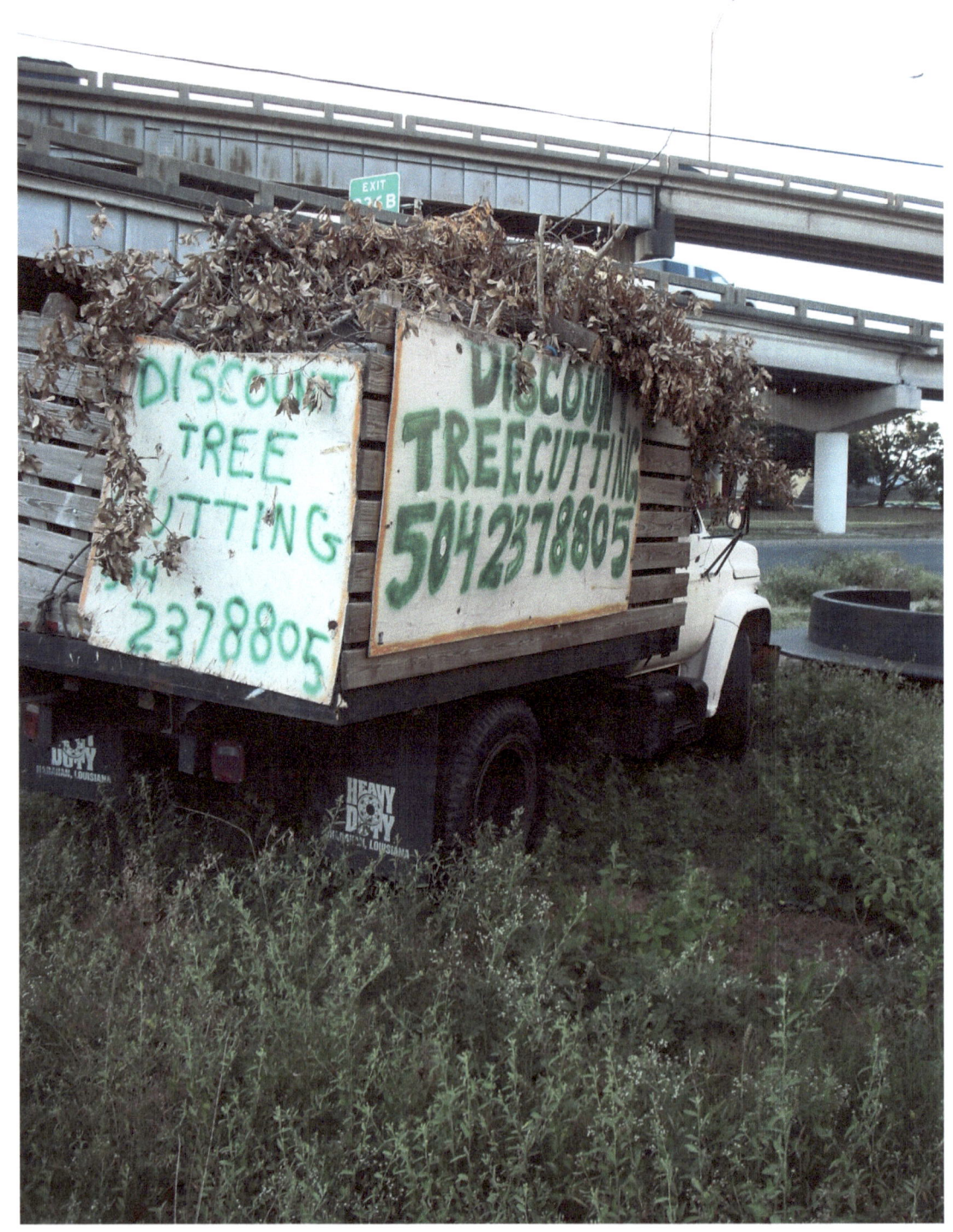

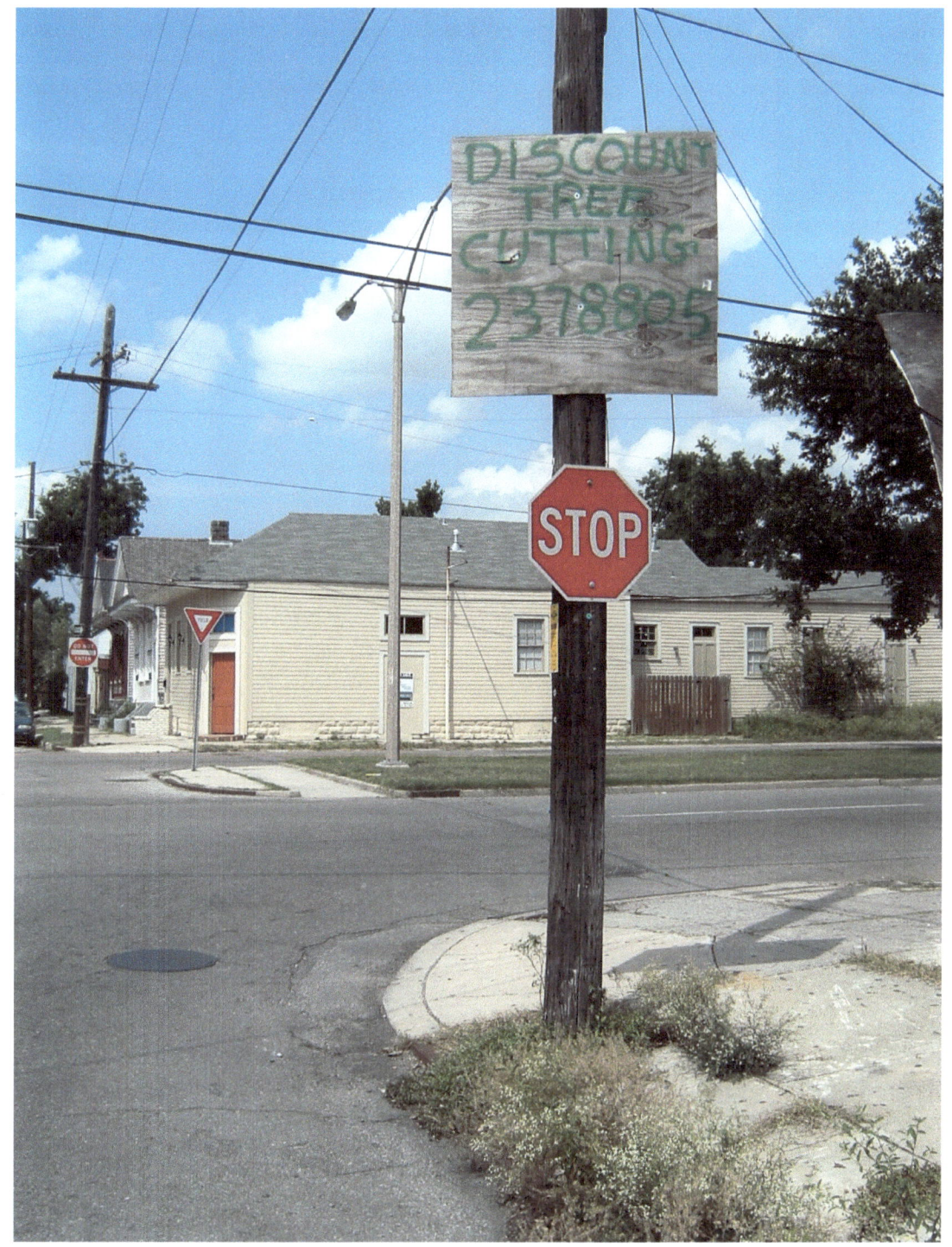

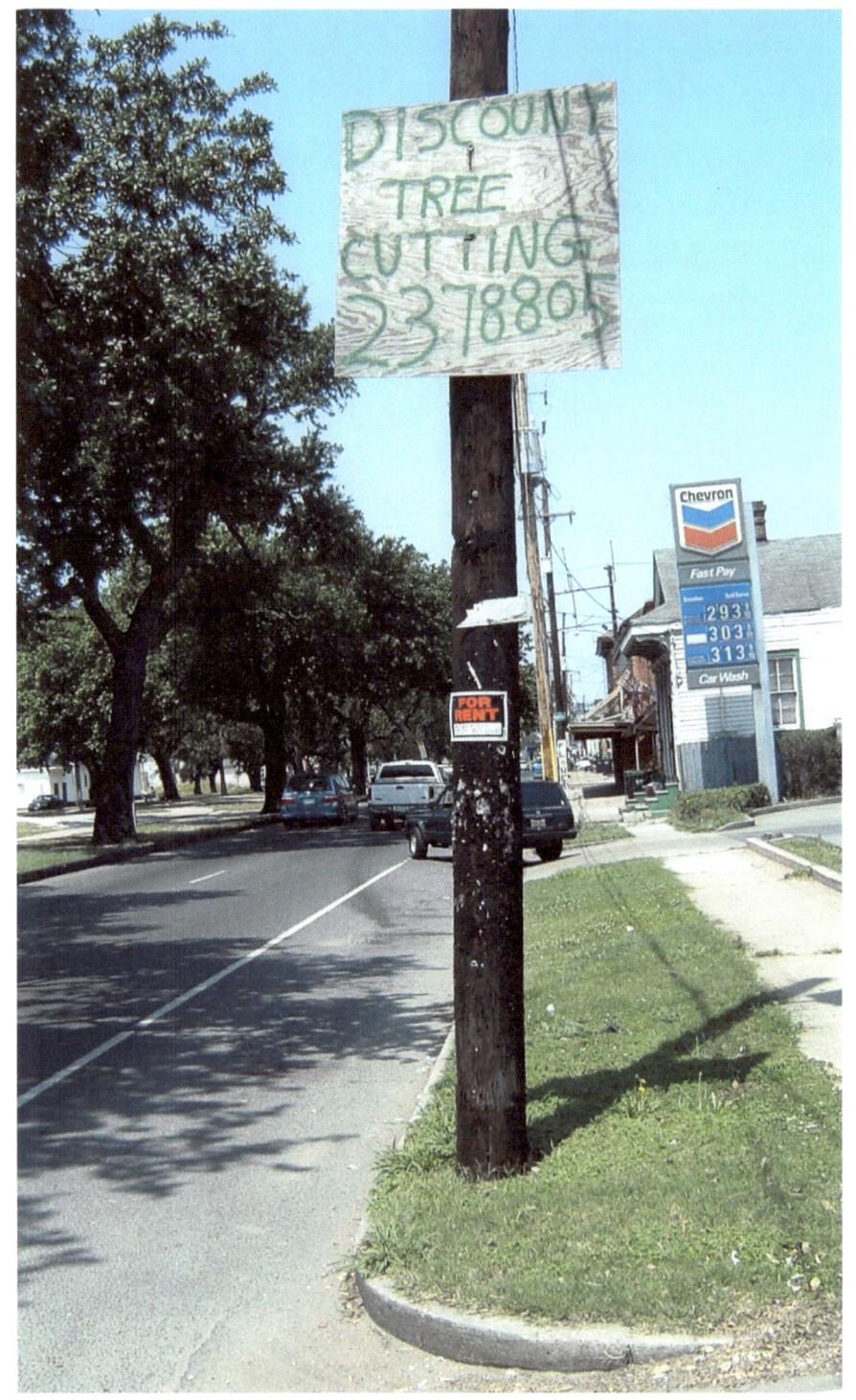

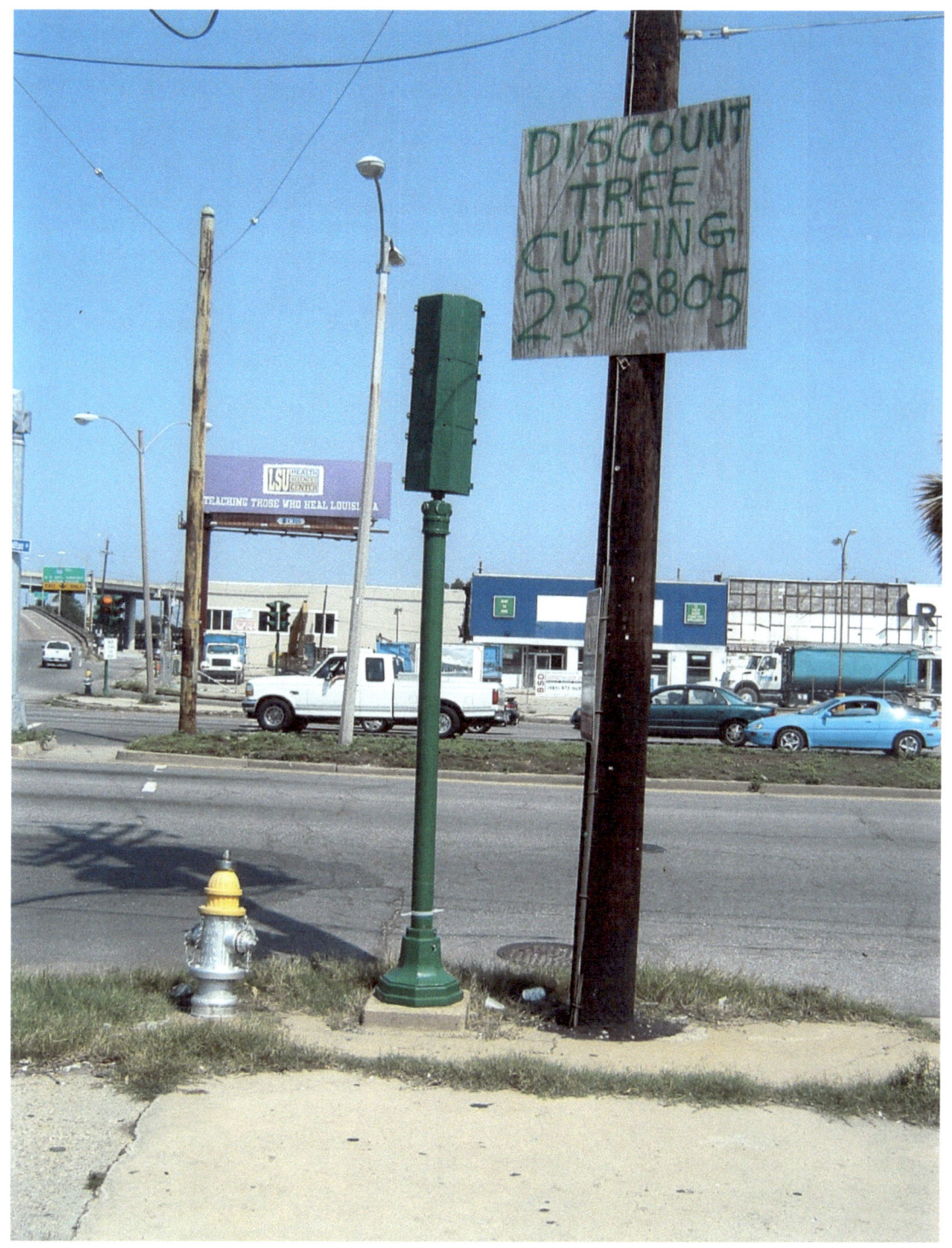

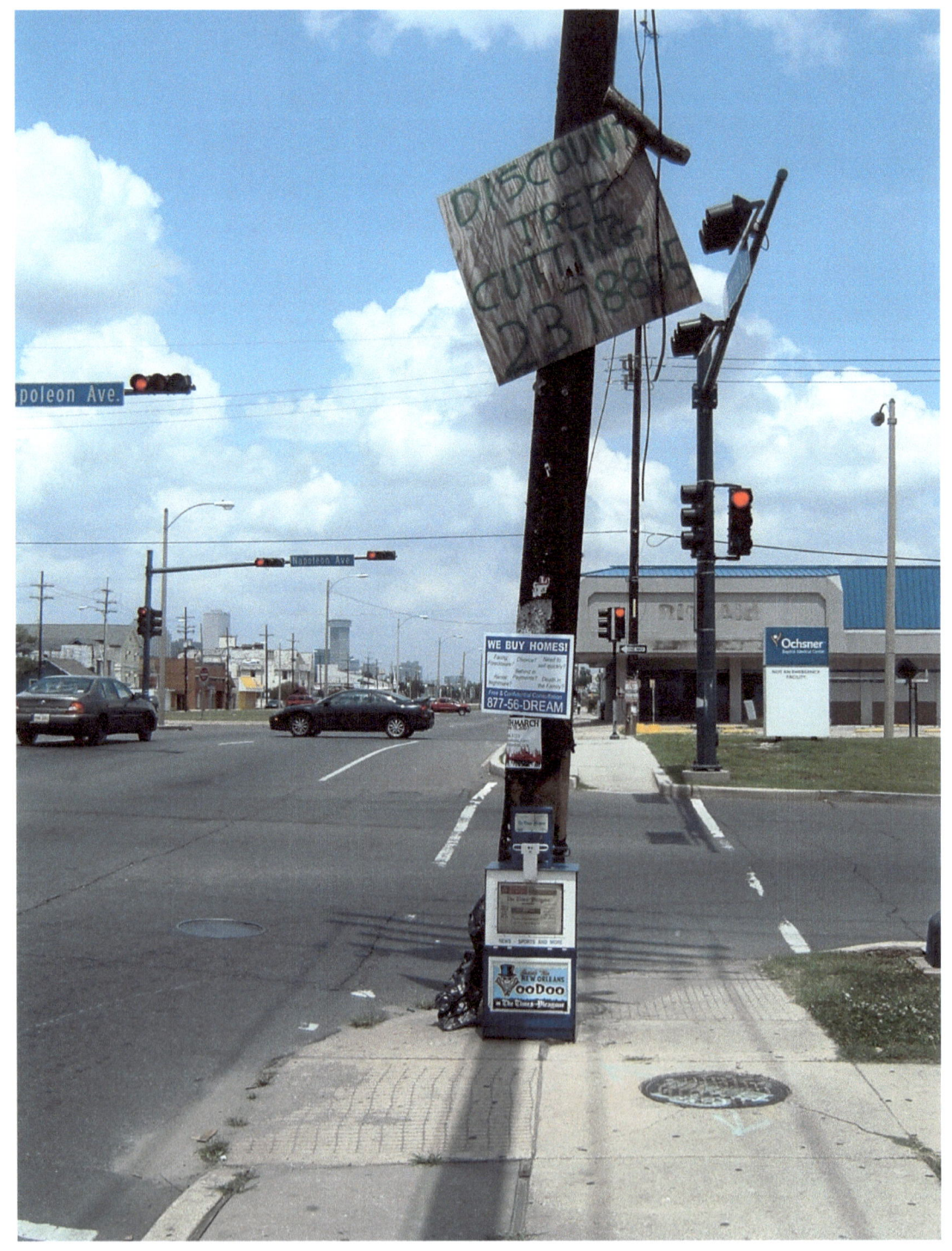

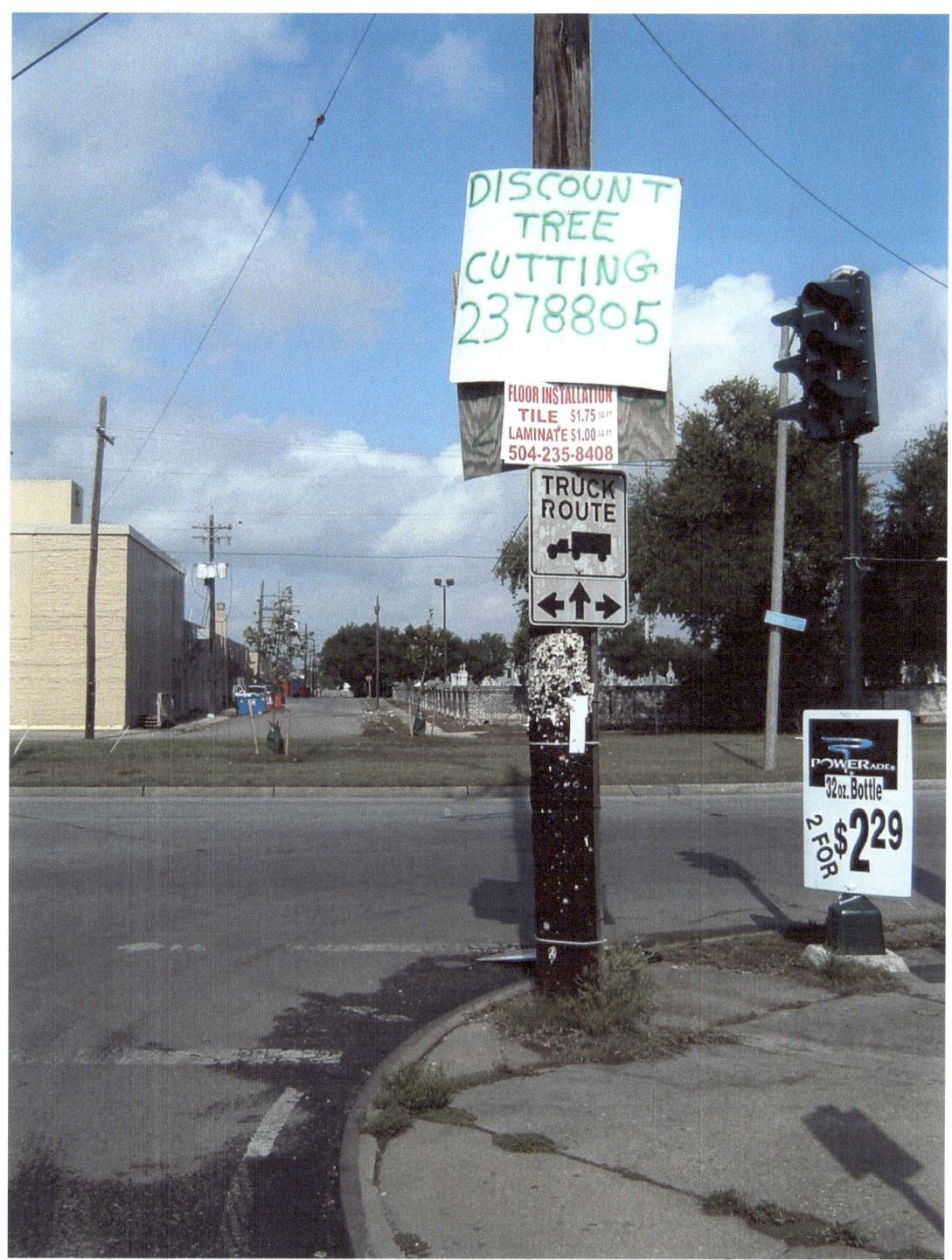

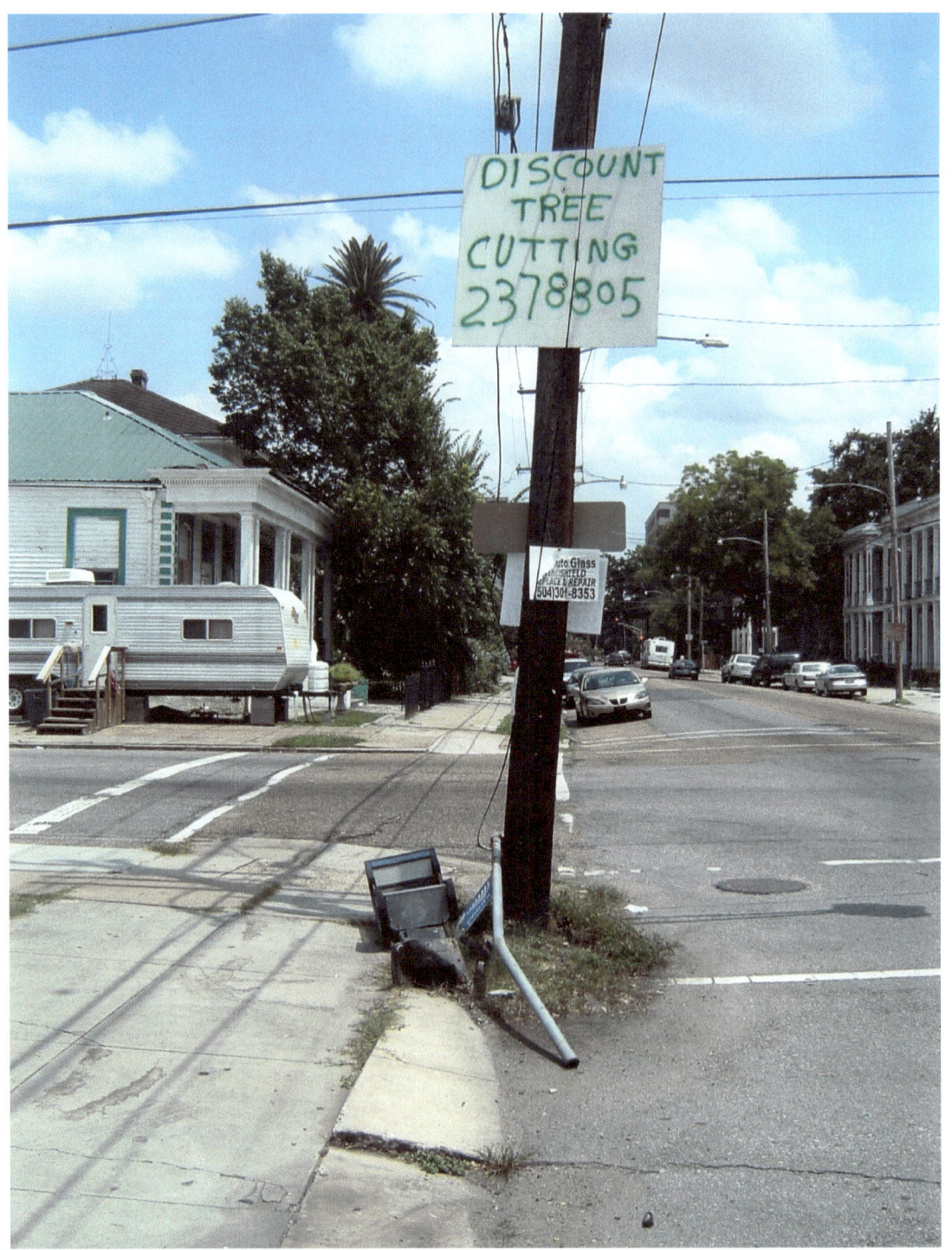

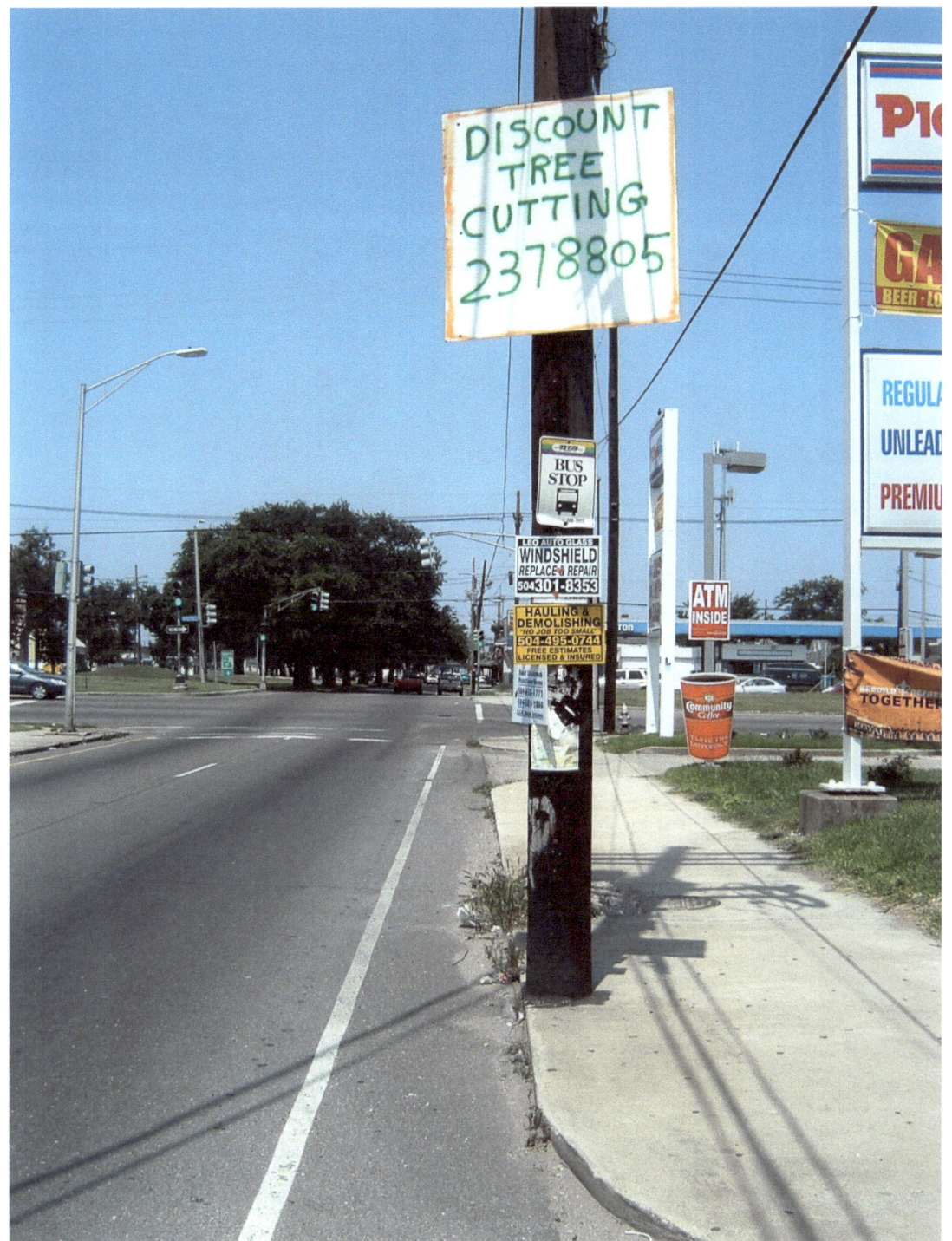

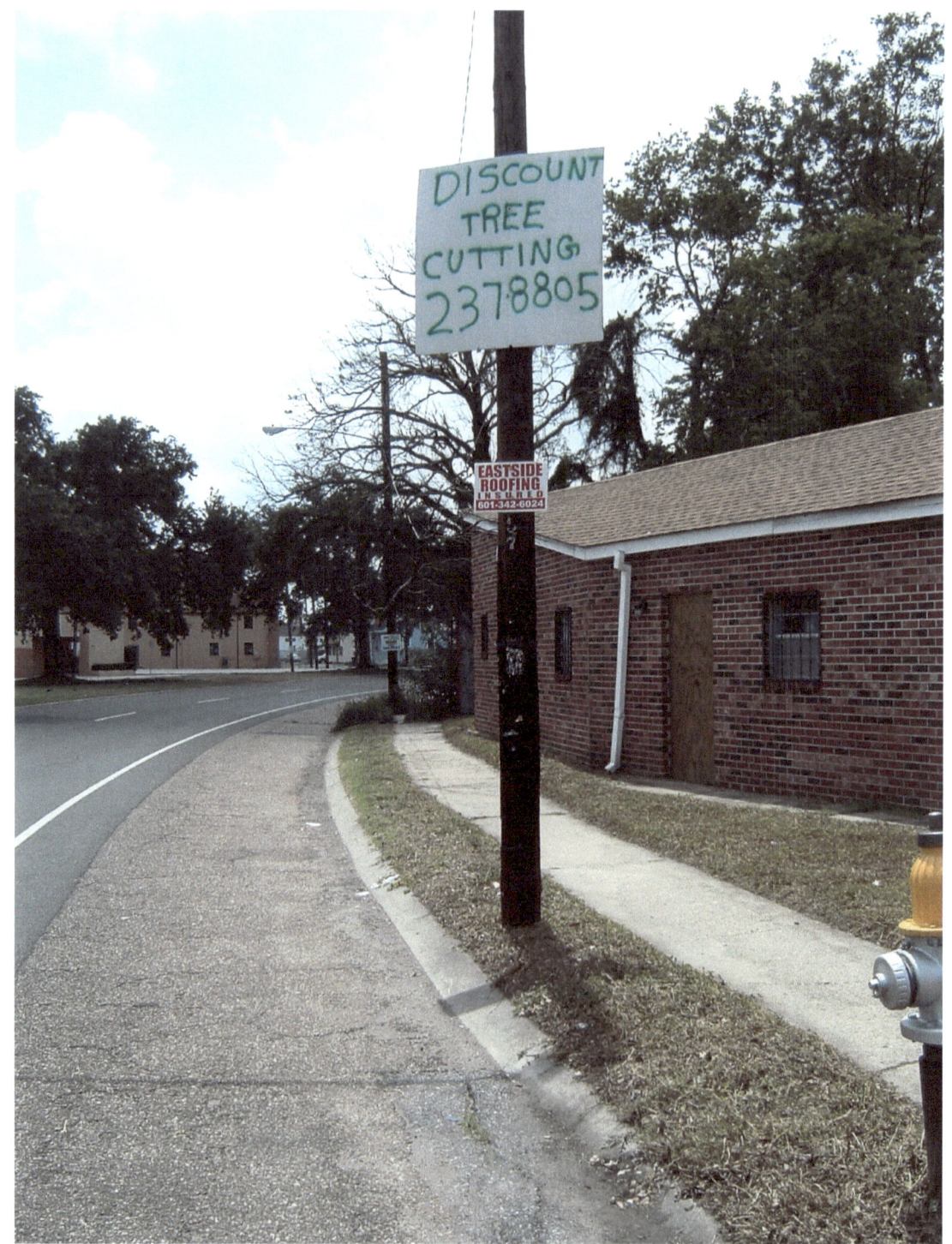

82

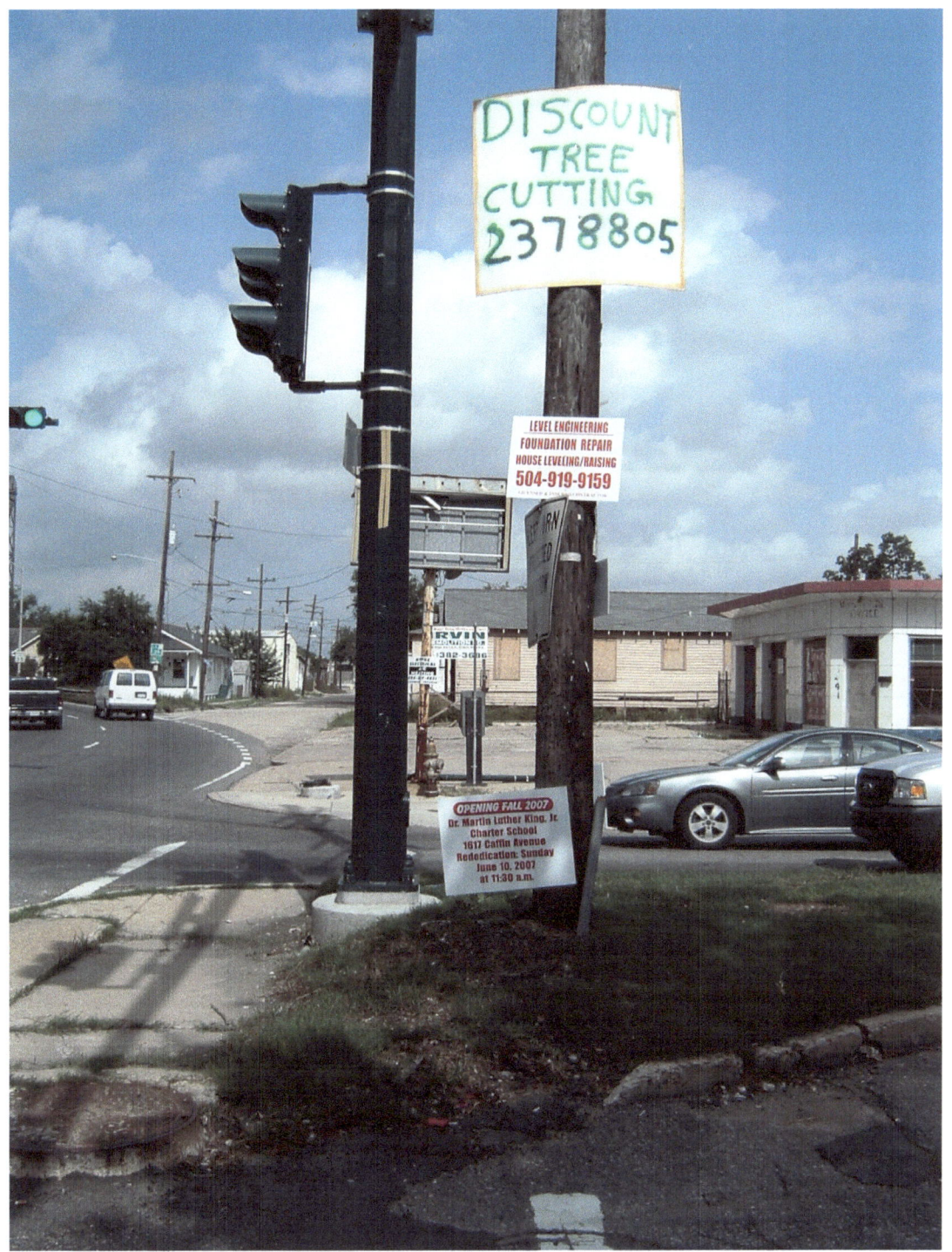

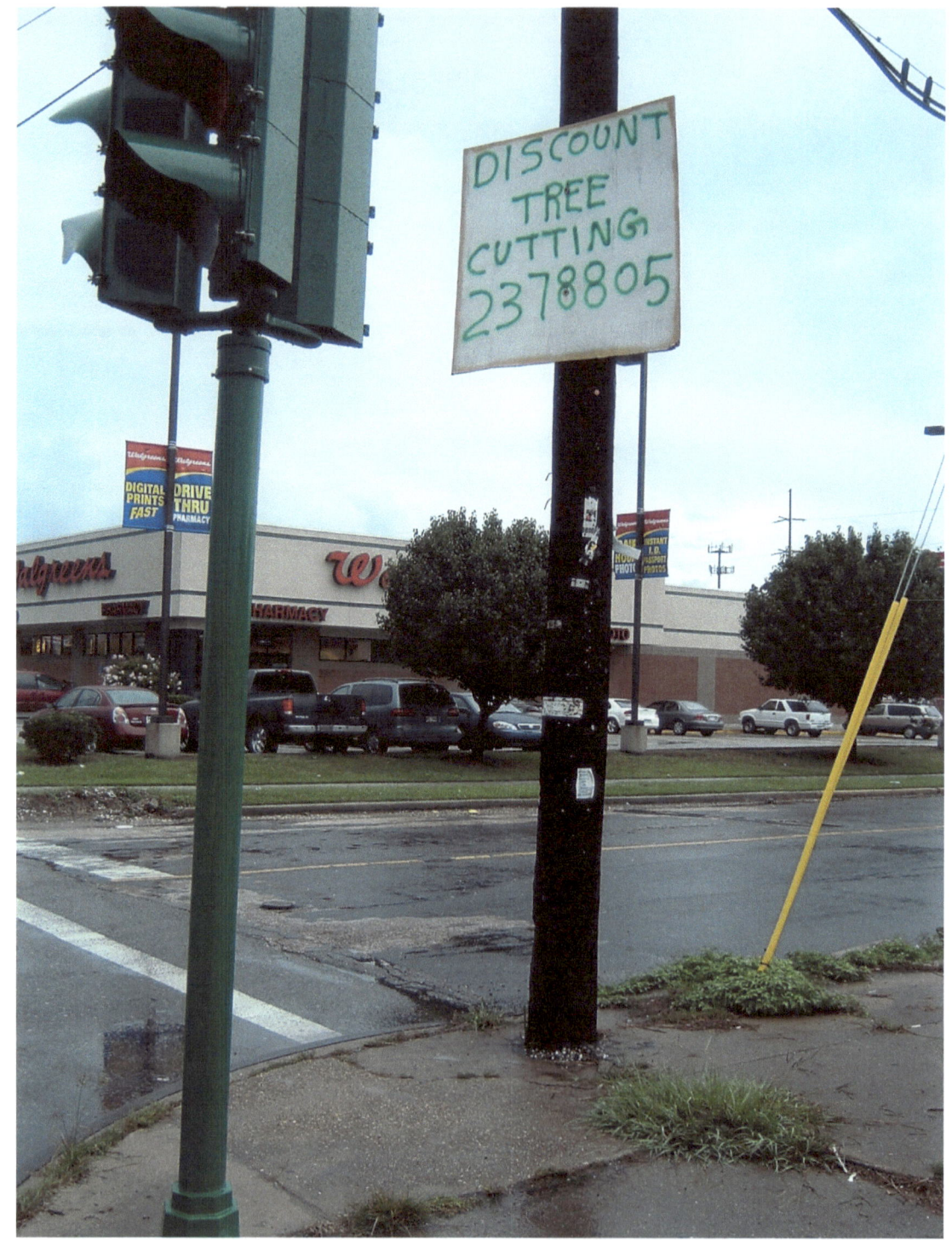

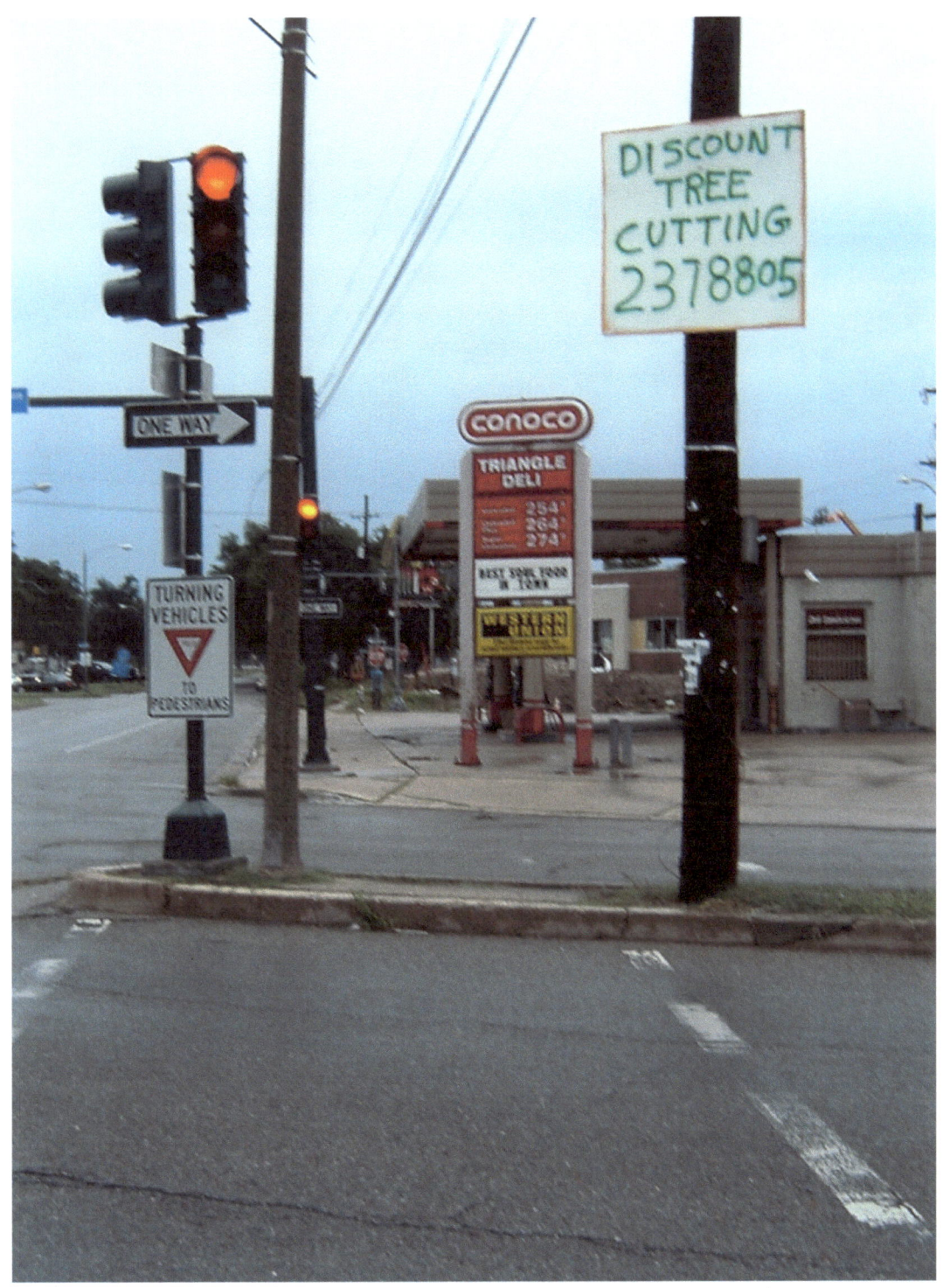

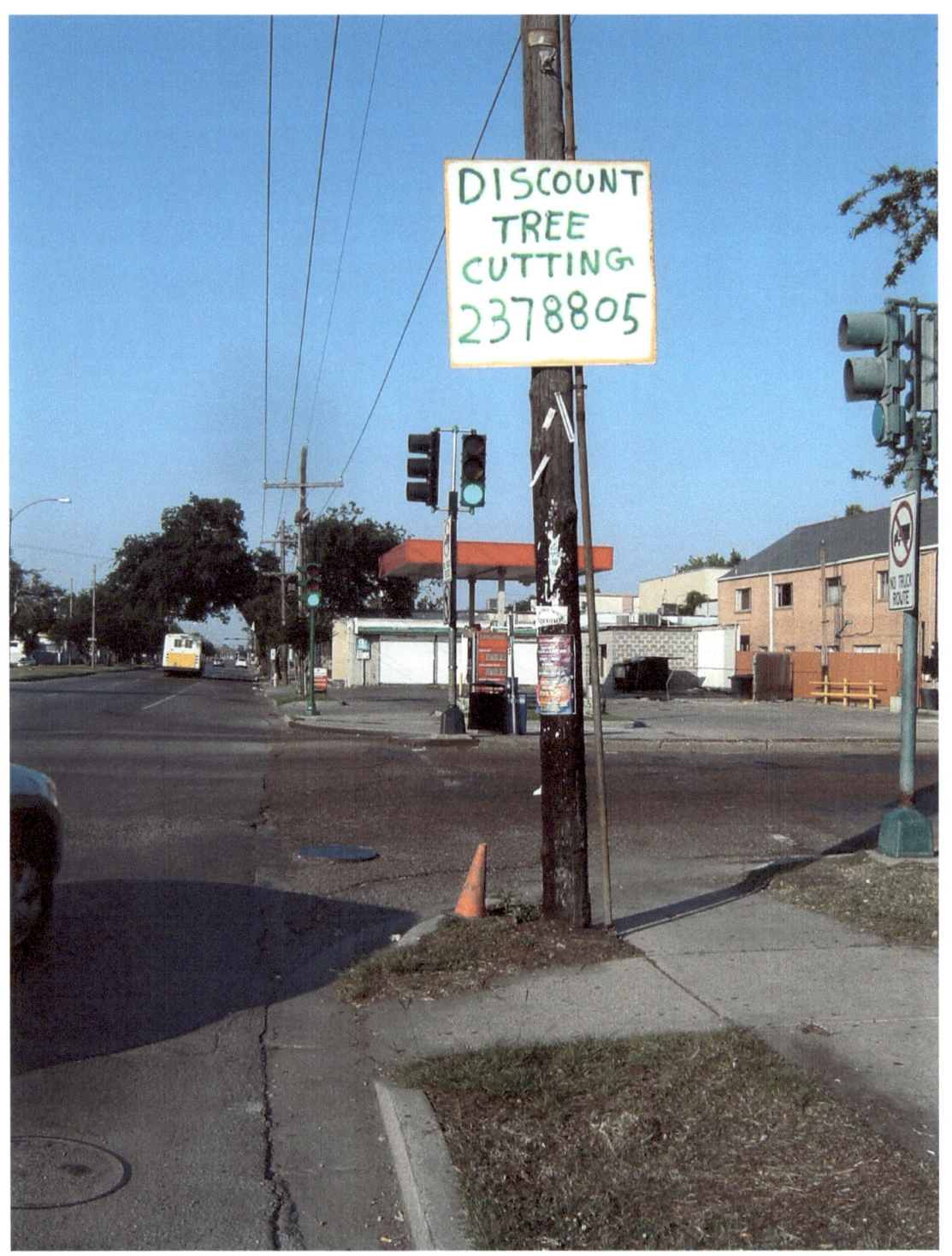

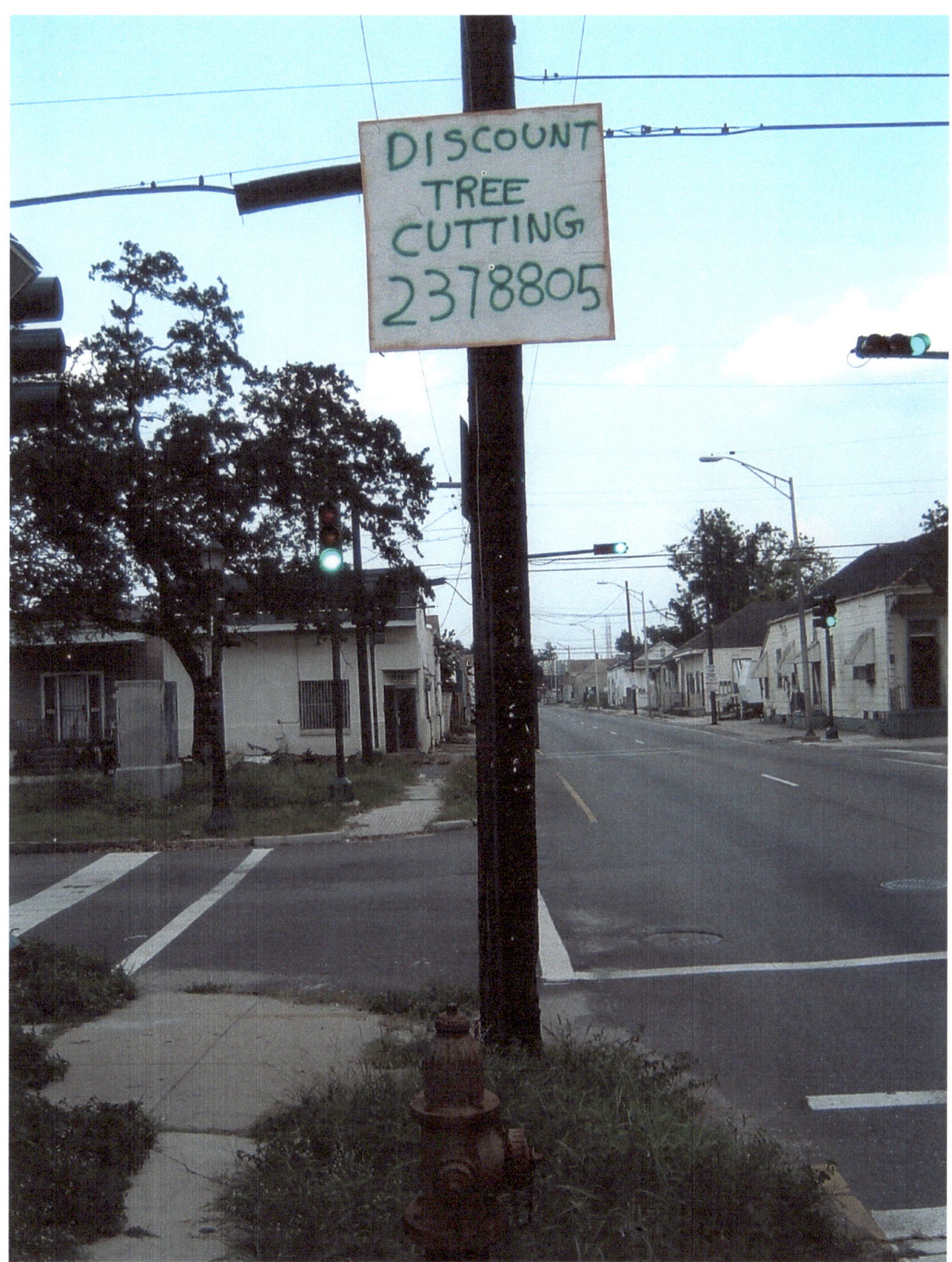

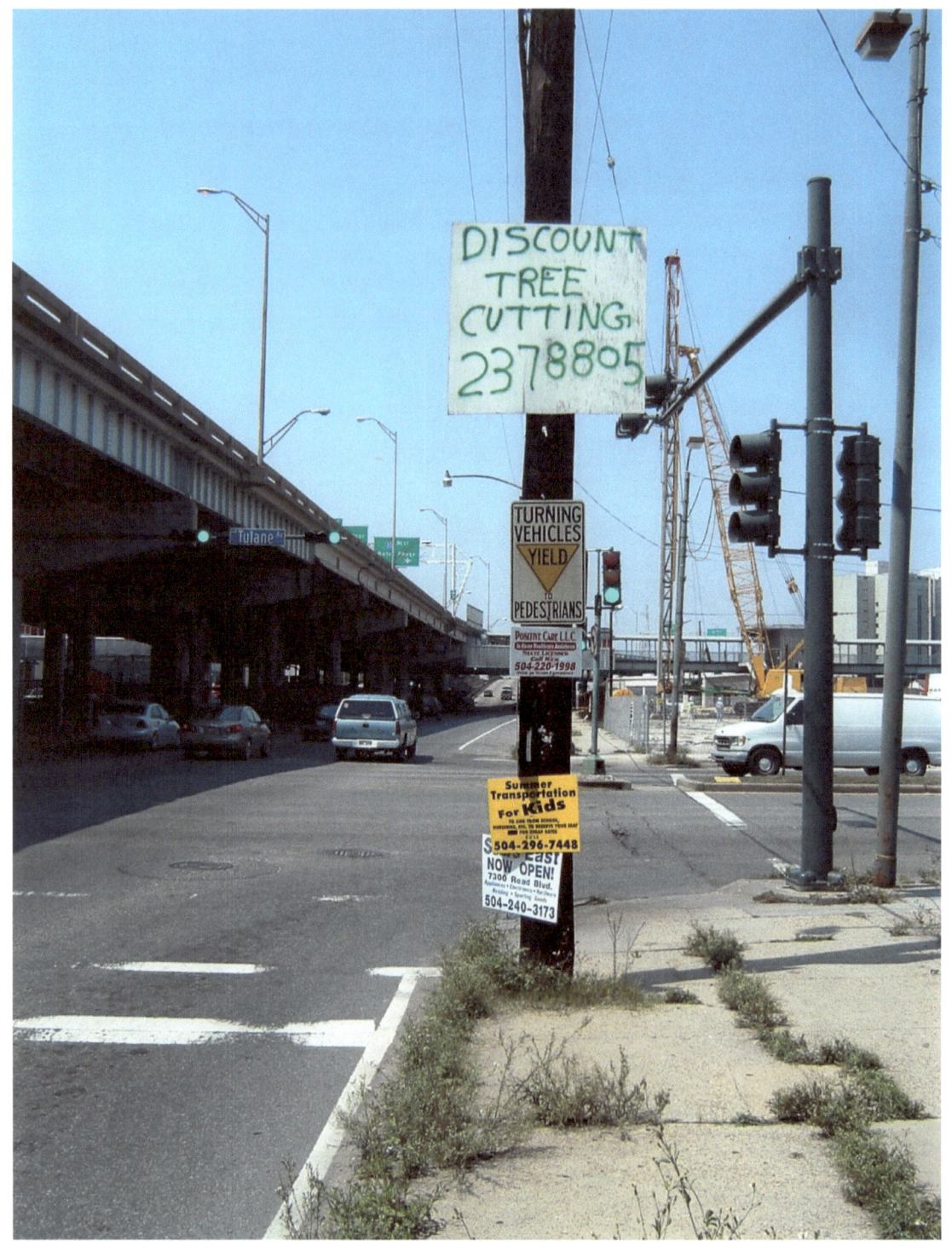

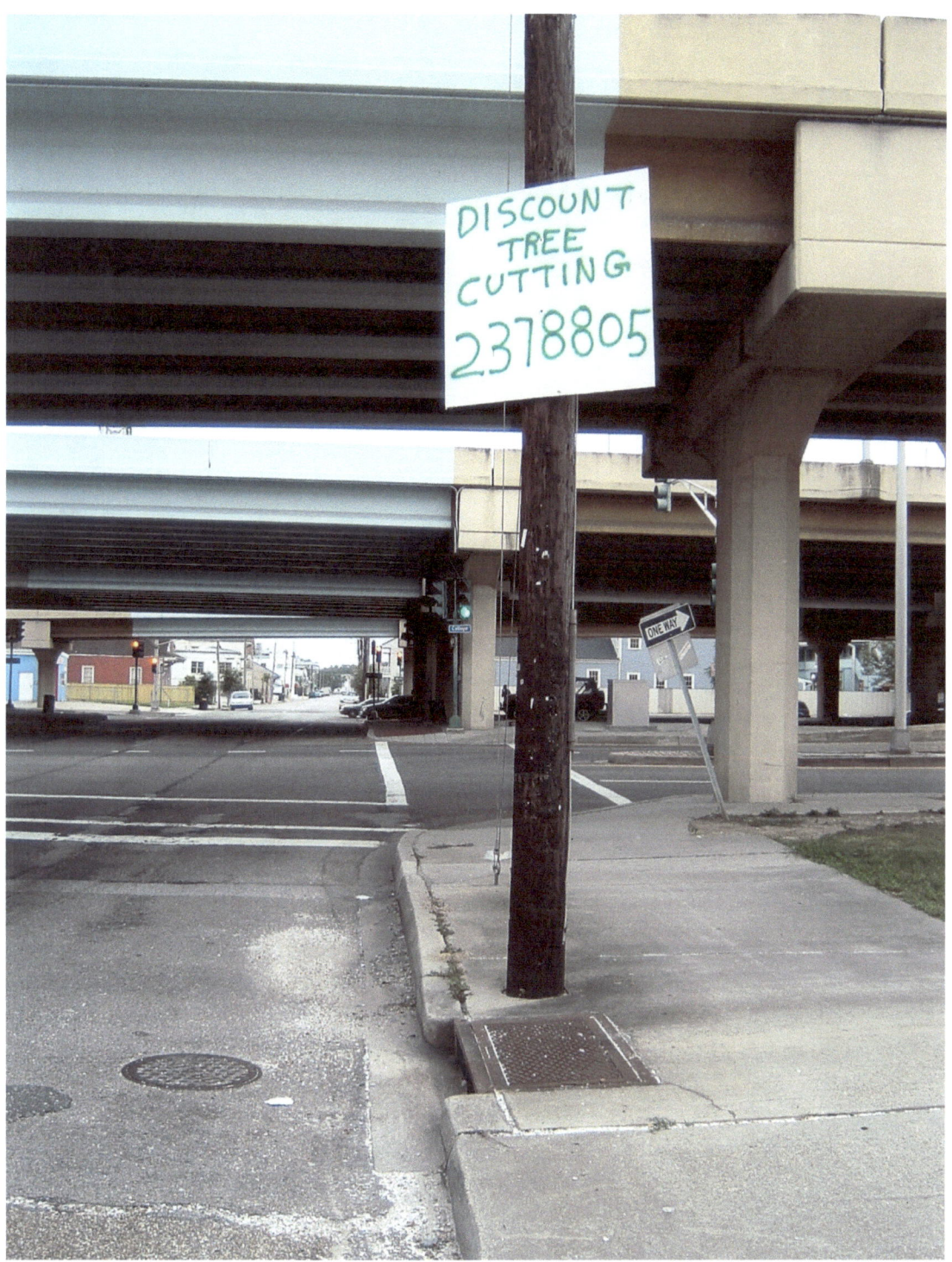

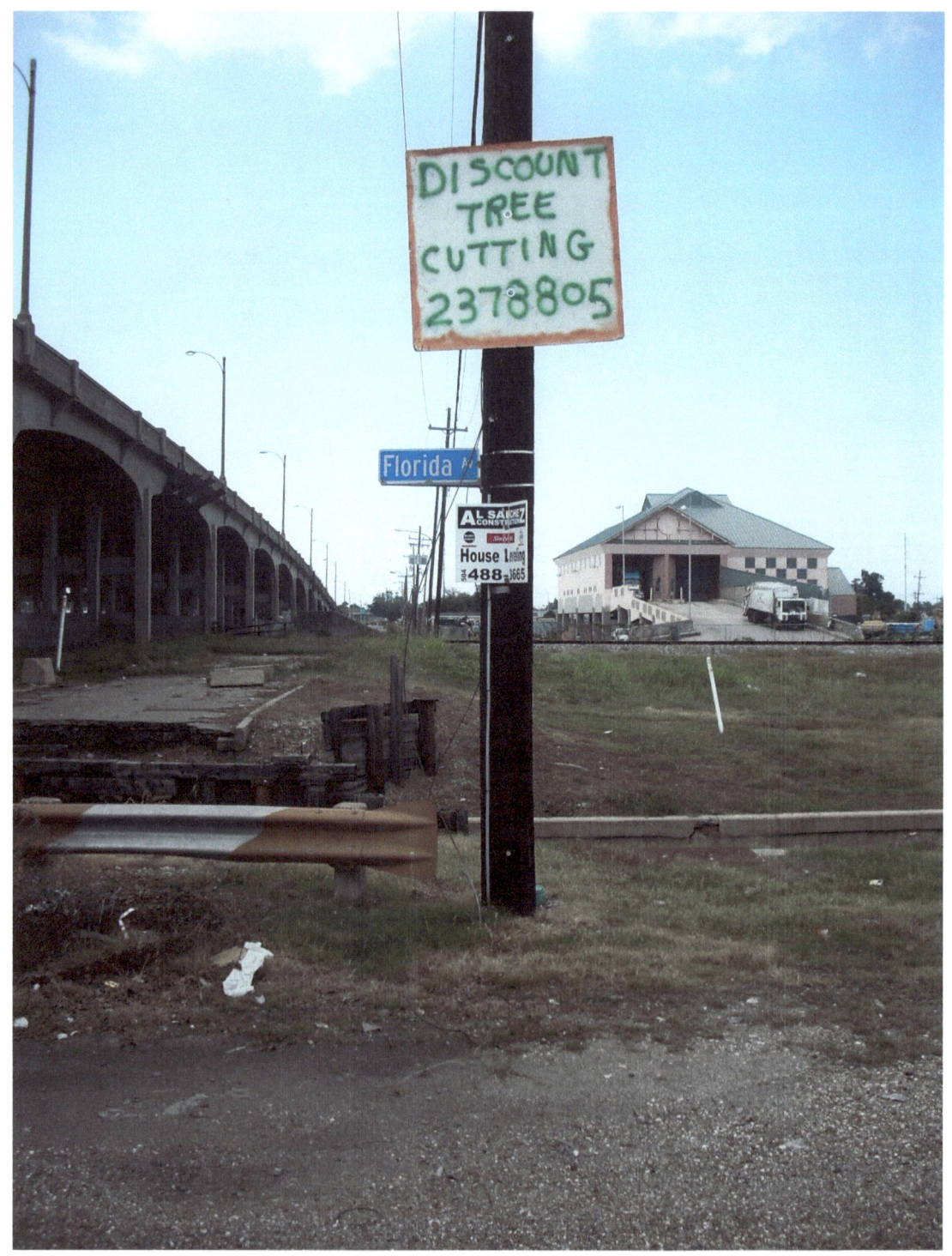

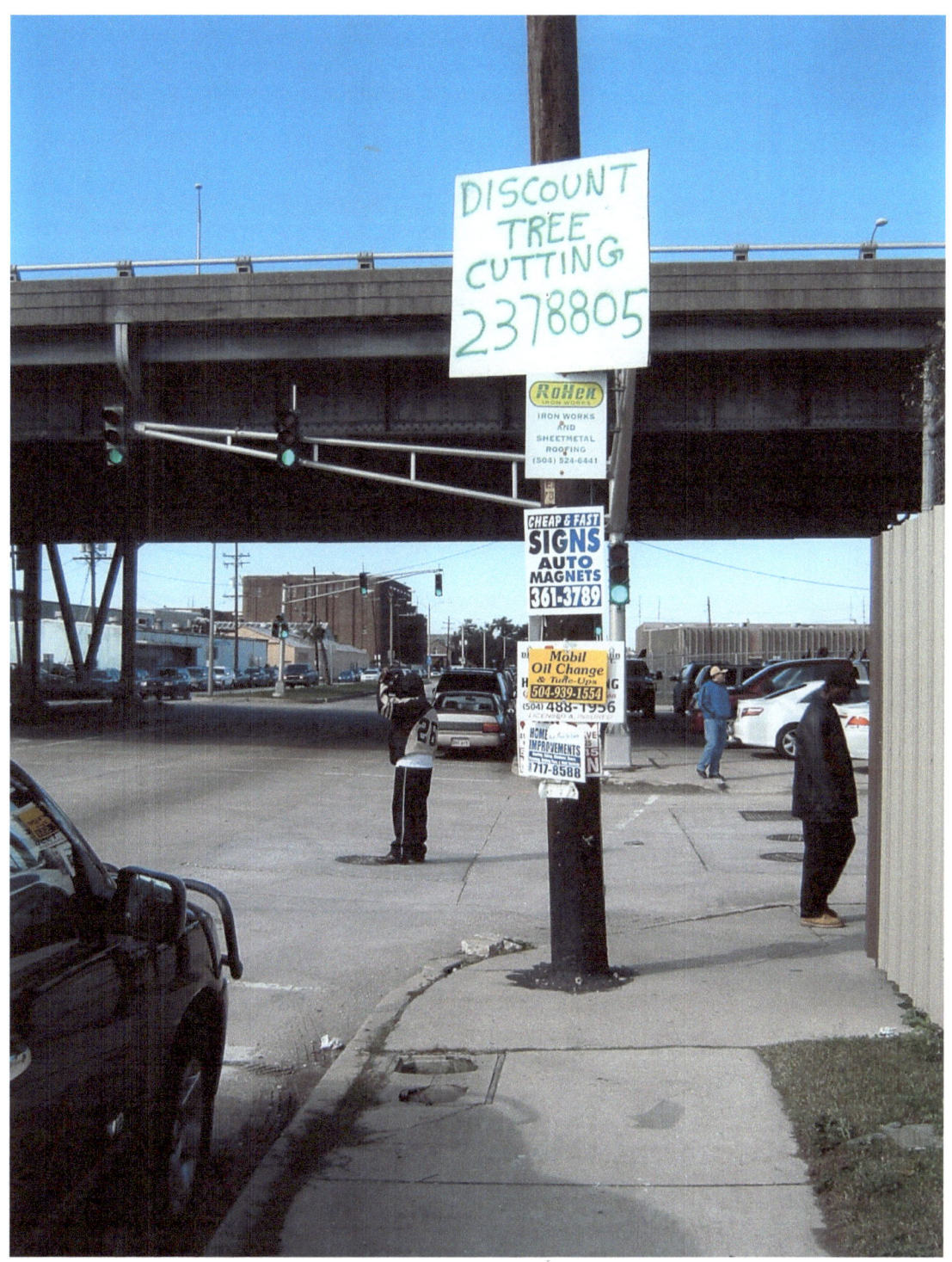

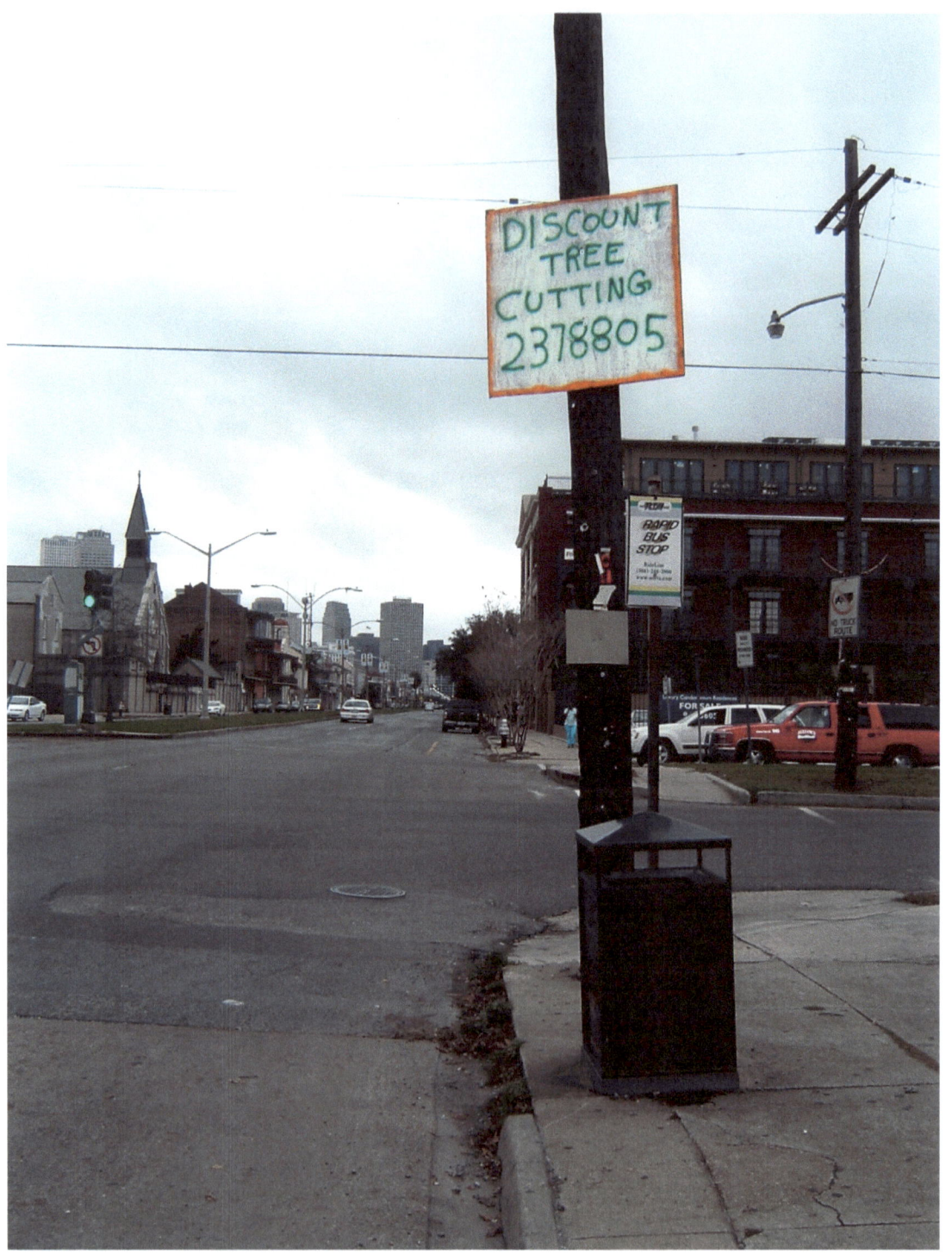

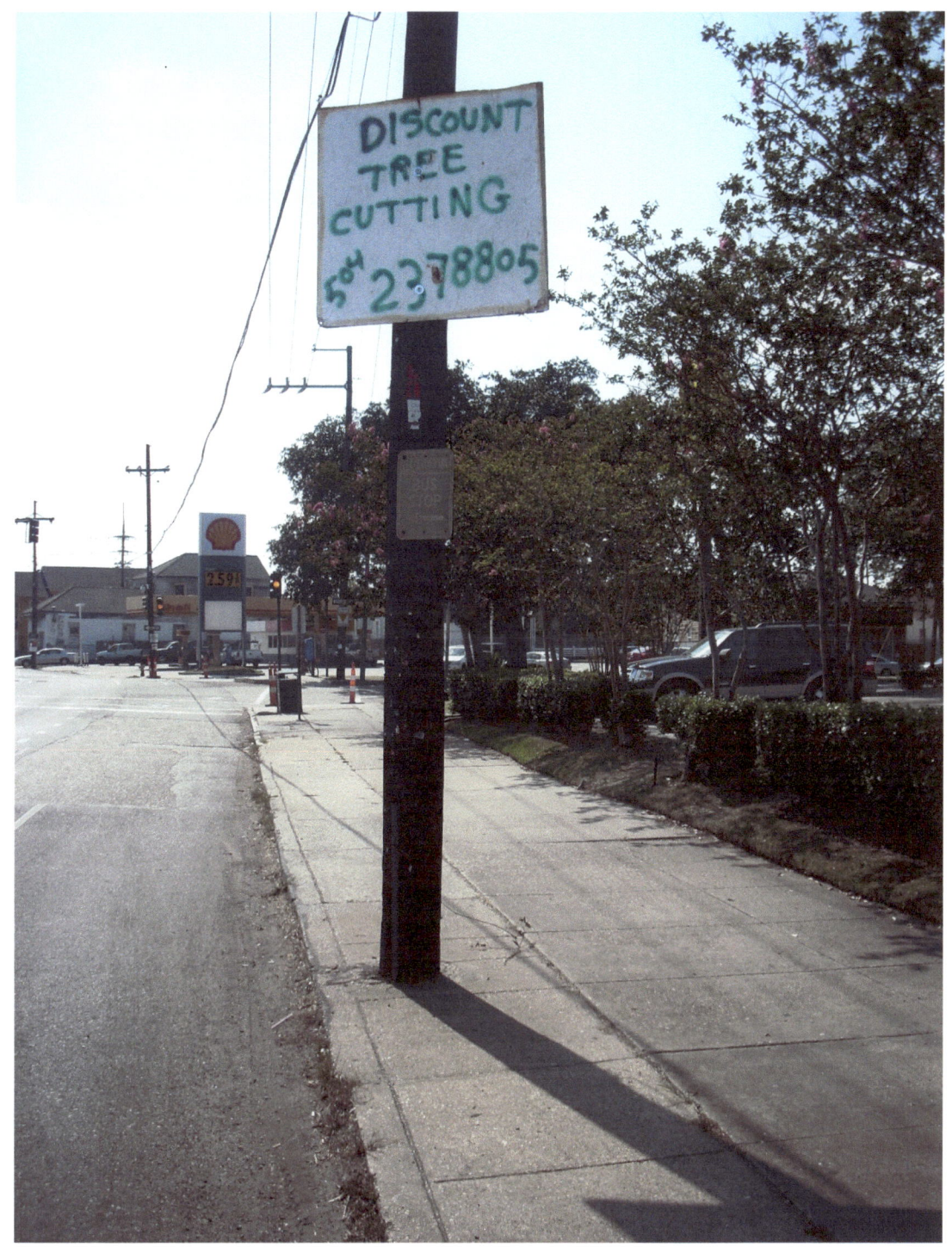

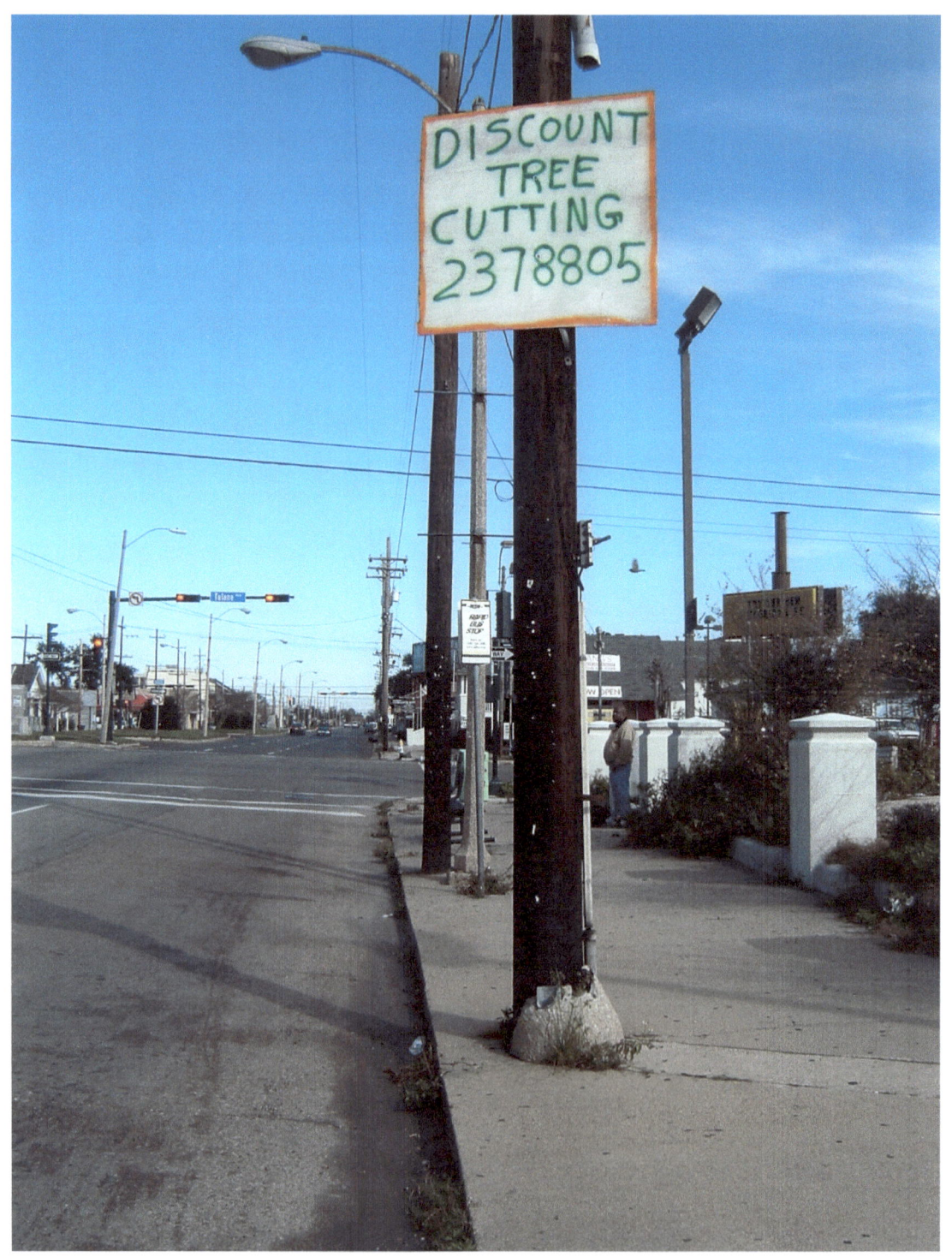

94

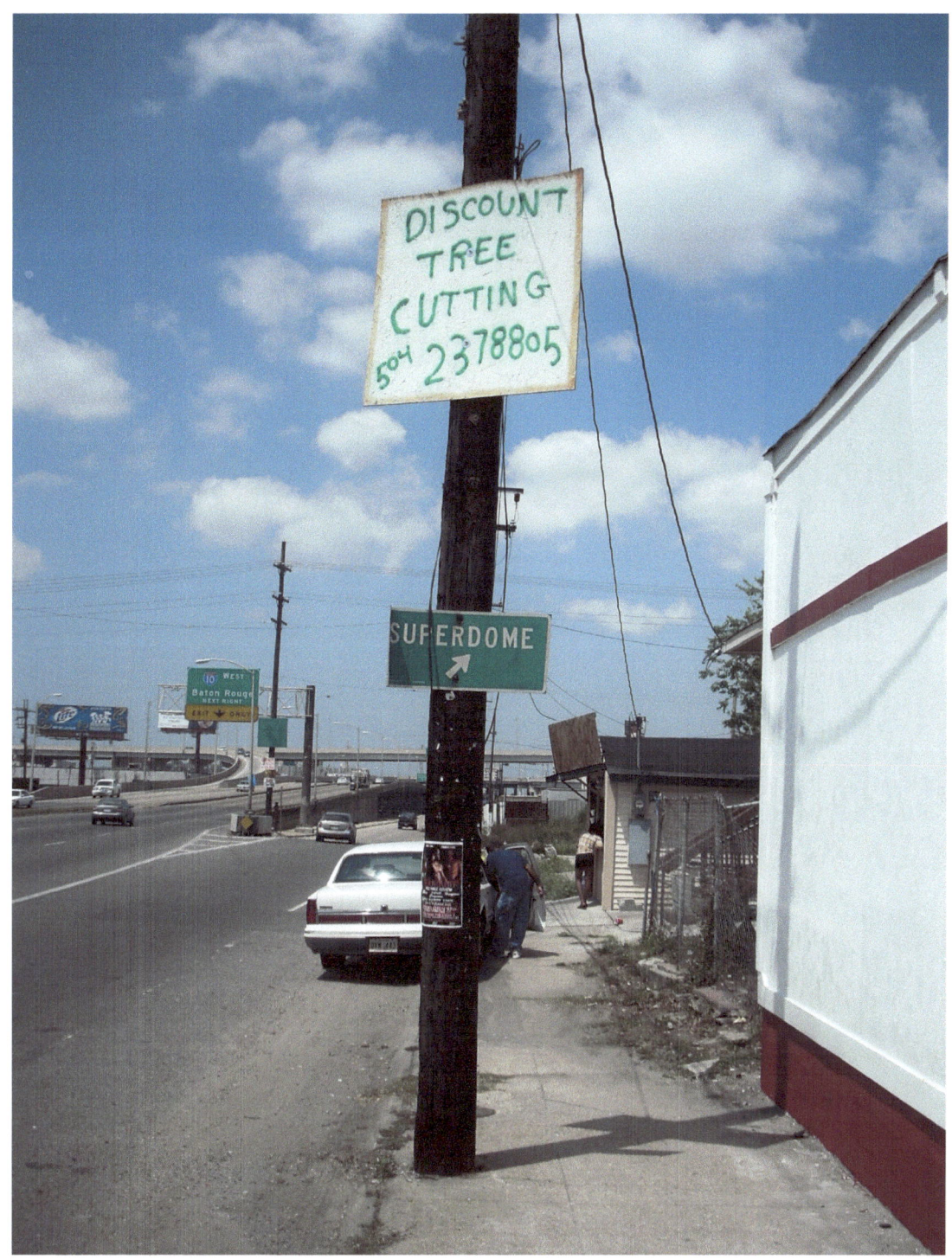

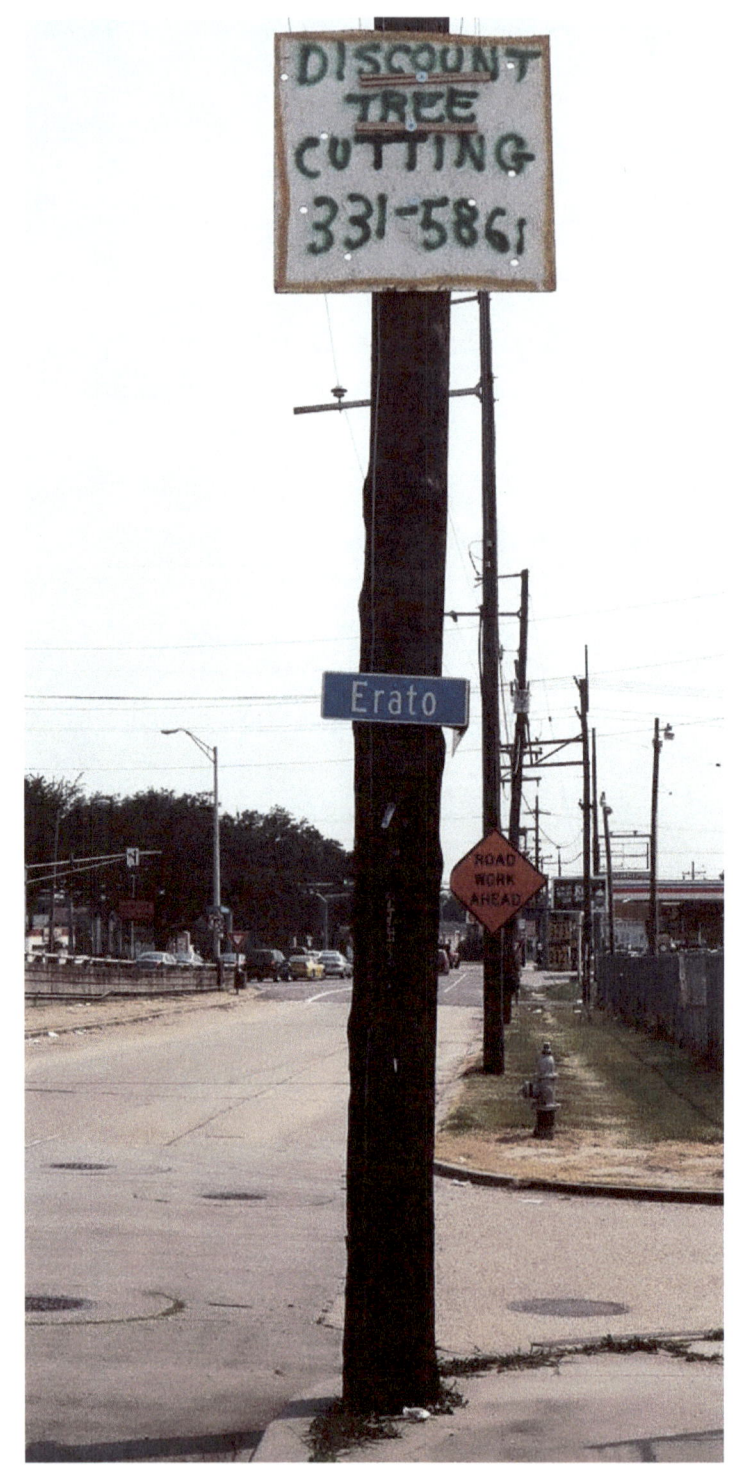

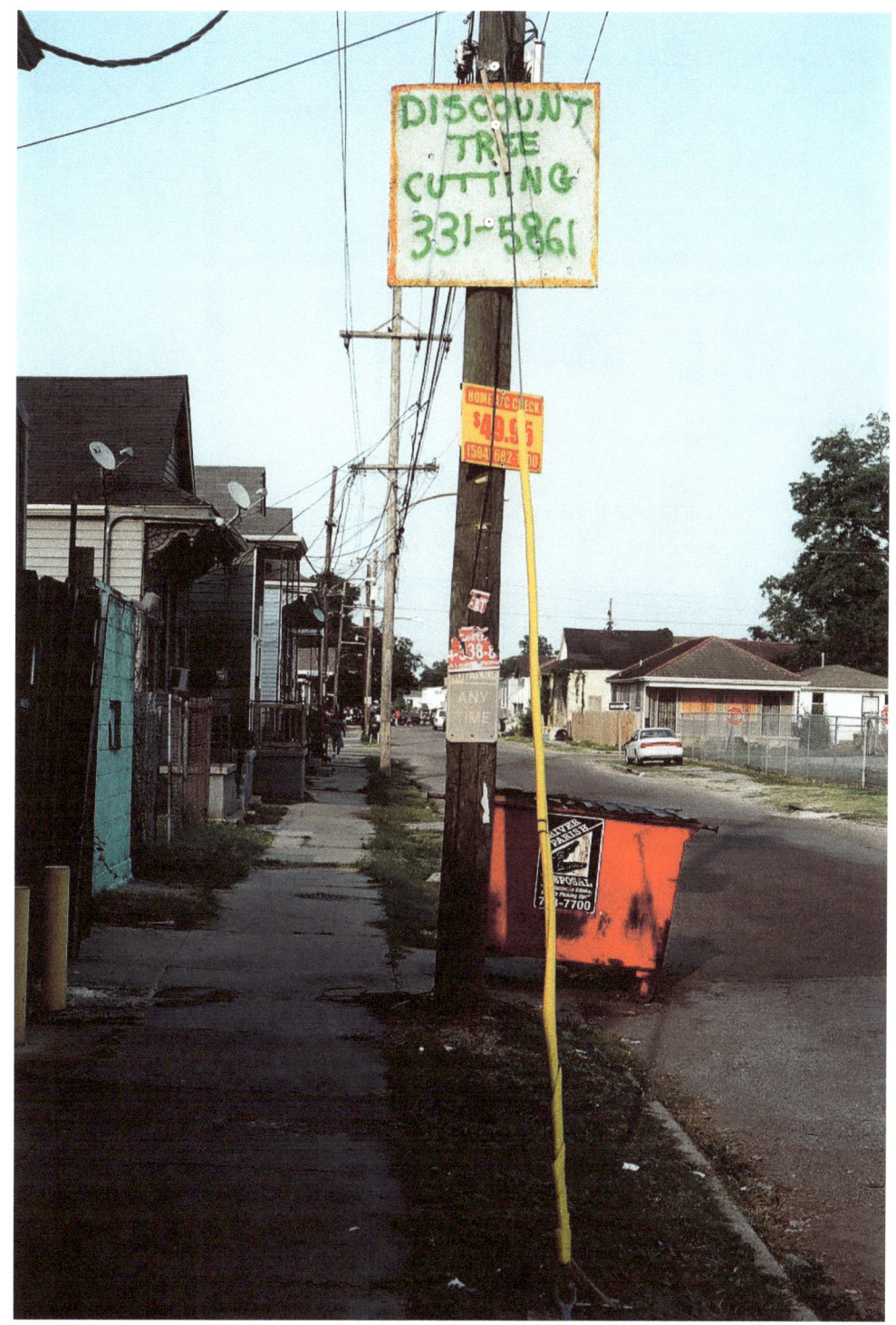

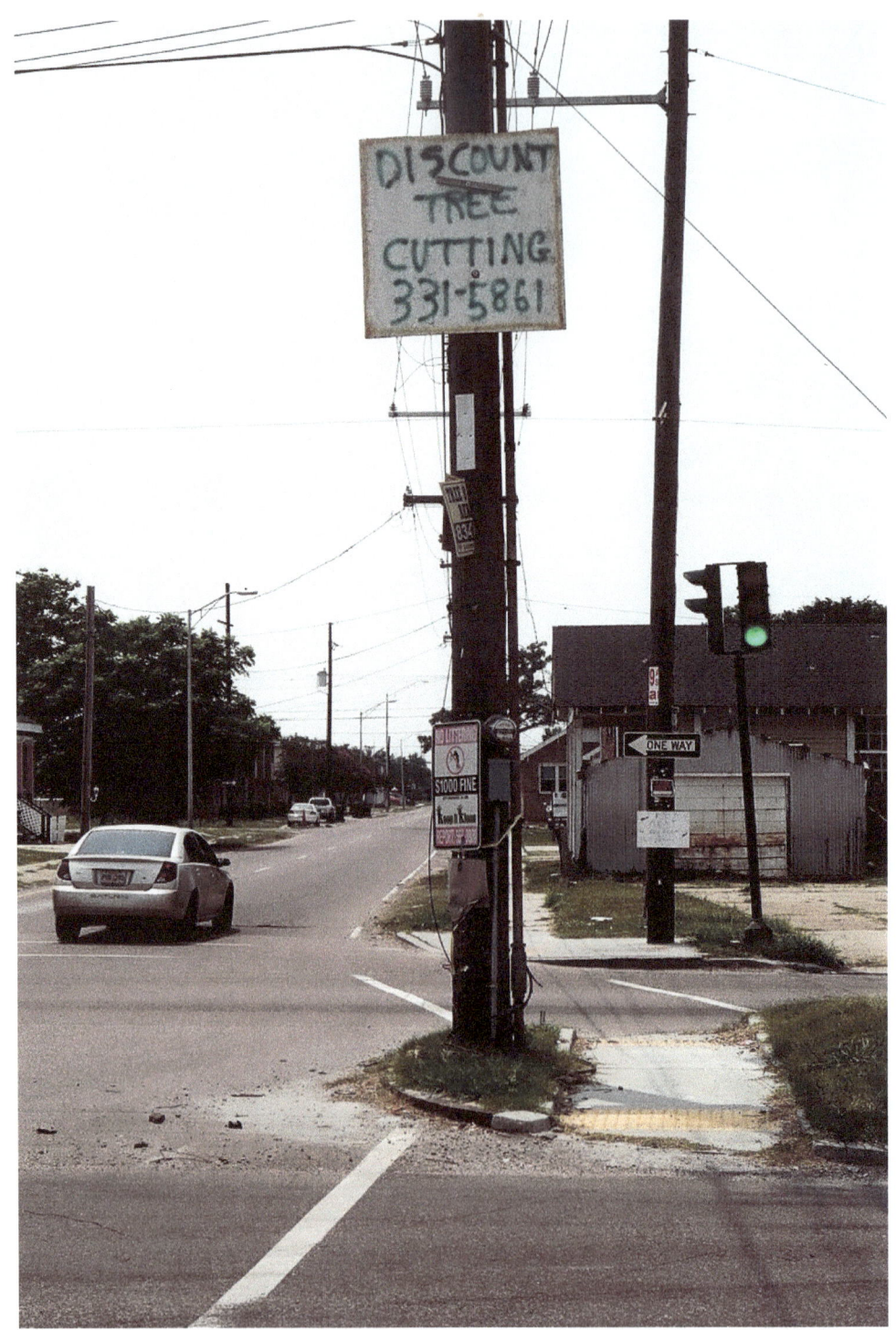

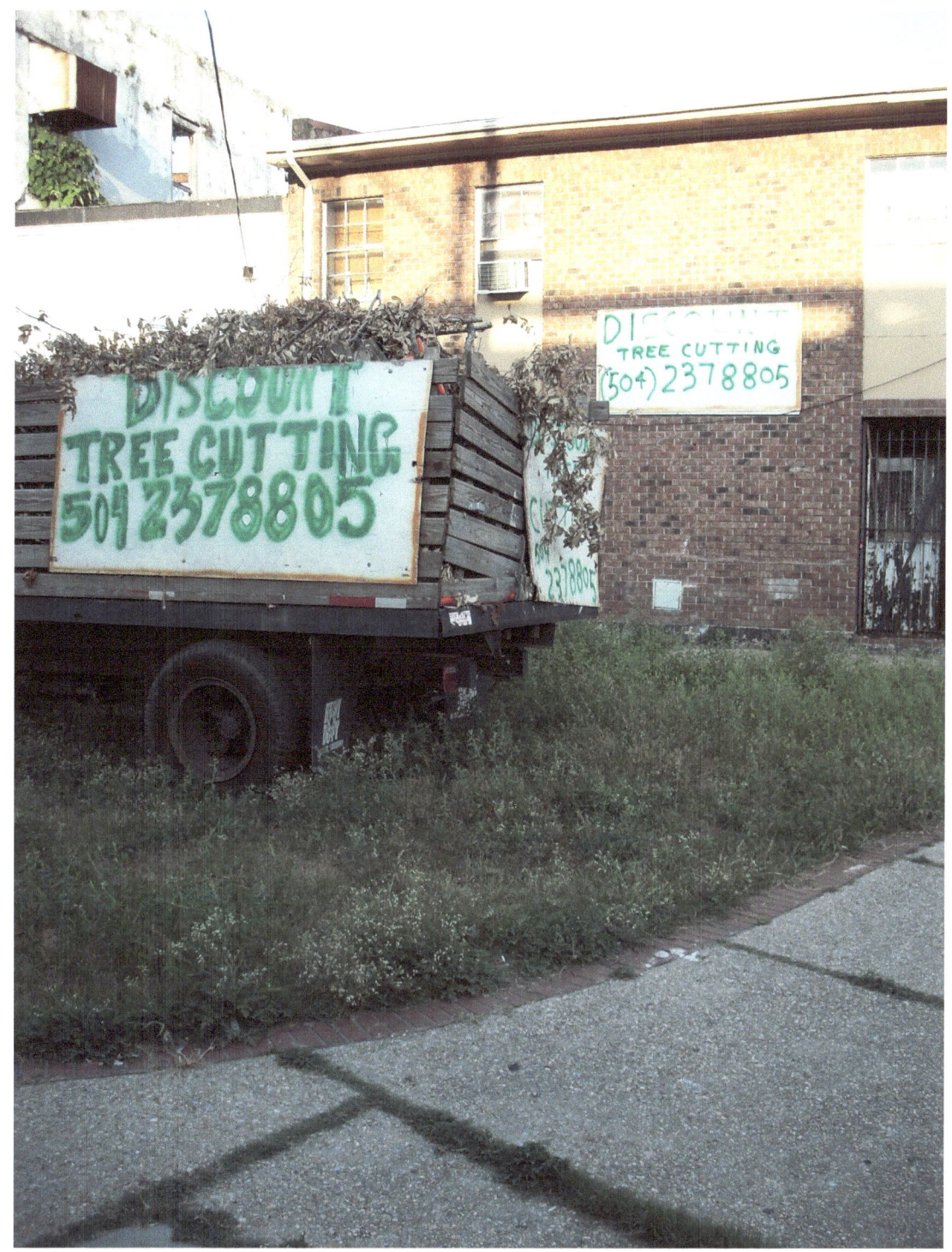

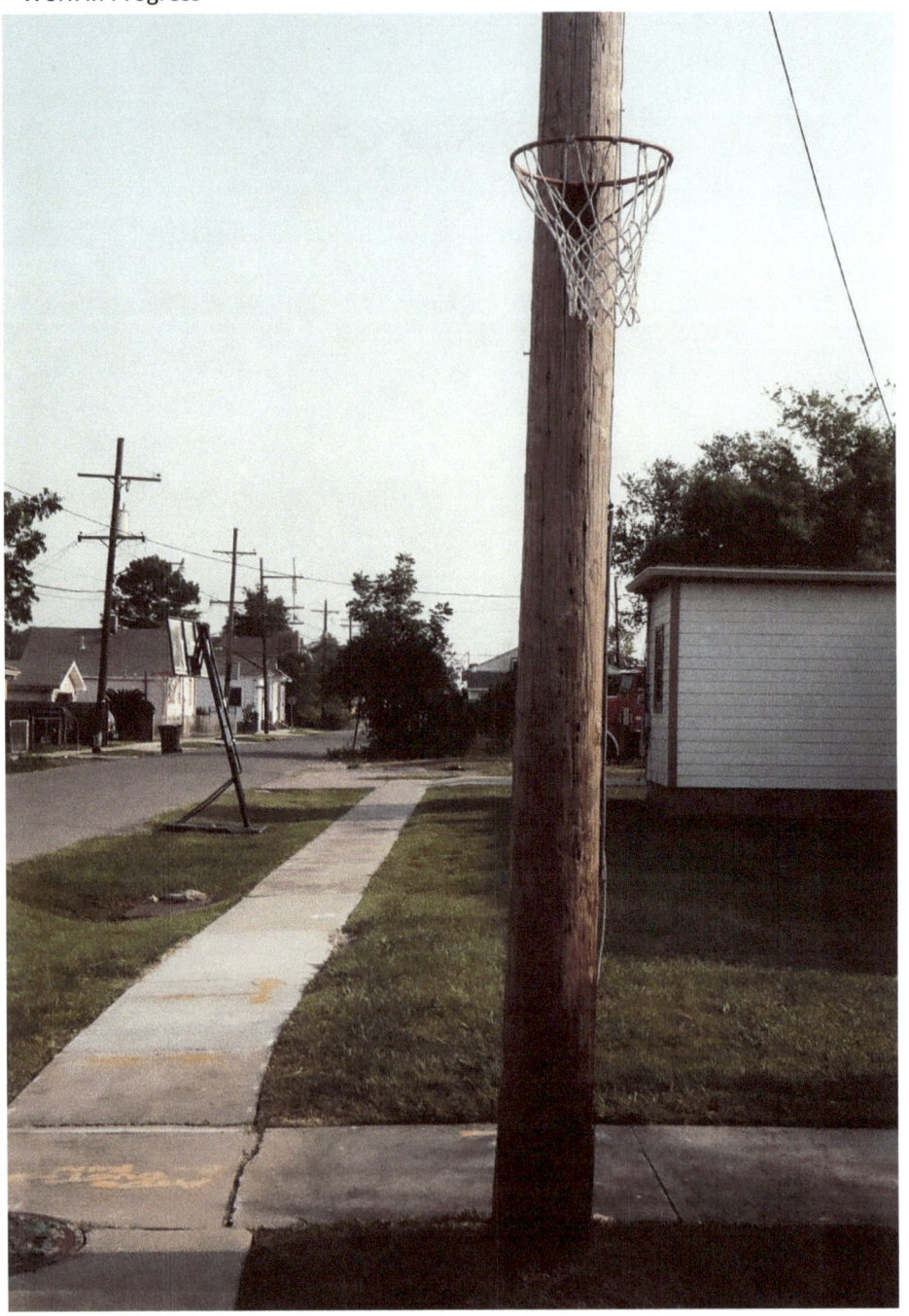

: DEPARTMENTS OF PARKS AND RECREATION NEW ORLEANS

Today I had to explain Language Photography to a pair of burglary detectives. At the salvage yard to recycle a washing machine. That's $6.78 for me, and I did a double take to notice a suited man wearing a badge behind the cashier at the pay window; got my money and left. Not far when I had to pull over and take pictures of a basketball hoop for a project called Departments of Parks and Recreation New Orleans. I took about a dozen with this joyless photon-recording device - a 10 year old $30.00 from Ebay-Nikon.

Returning to the Corolla, and the detectives have pulled over:

- What you doing?

- Taking pictures of that basketball hoop.

- What's that for?

- I like to take pictures of hoops put up for kids.

- Yeah, can I see?

He pointed to the camera.

Just like that, I consent search.

- Sure.

I hand it to him

He hands it back and says

- How do you replay?

I fumble with large dumb hands pawing inscrutable buttons that are small and new to me. His partner says

- Is that your camera?

- Yeah. I don't know these digital things very well.

- I was raised on film.

- Back in the day developing and stuff.

- Yeah

- Didn't you come out of the salvage yard?

- Yeah, my washer took a dive and I dismantled it to bring here.

- Come here a lot?

- Just when I have junk to recycle.

By now his partner is scrolling through my pictures.

Yes a lot of hoops.

Then pictures of my van.

 - You take pictures of cars too?

- That's my van, its being towed to the junkyard tomorrow.

And he keeps going back: my socks on a clothes line, copy stand views of

Slight Publications books & Discount Tree Cutting signs...

hands it back and says

- A nice hobby huh?

- Yes

- Alright

- Thank you officers, as I always say to armed authorities.

Yes I hate that camera. I do love my hobby though.

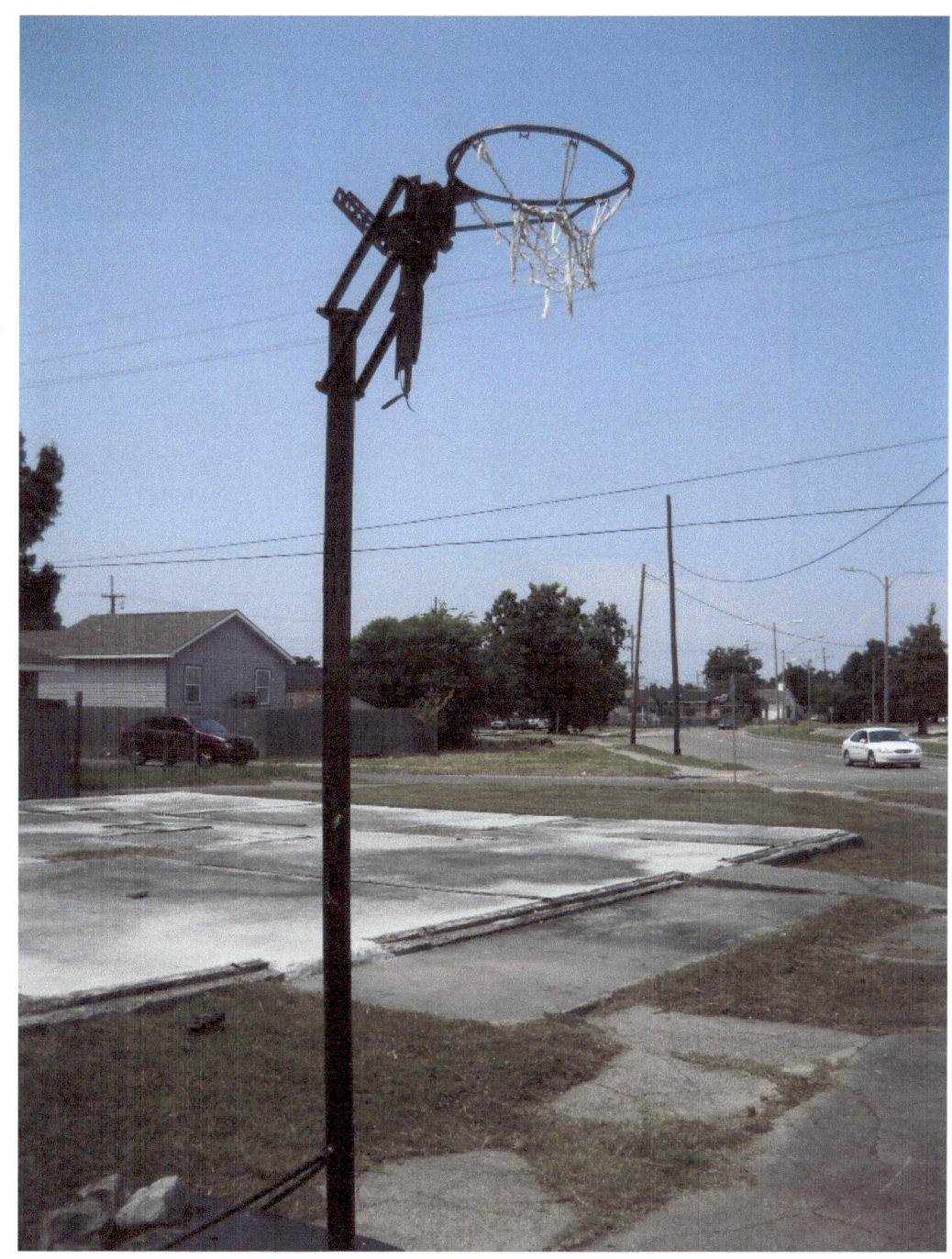

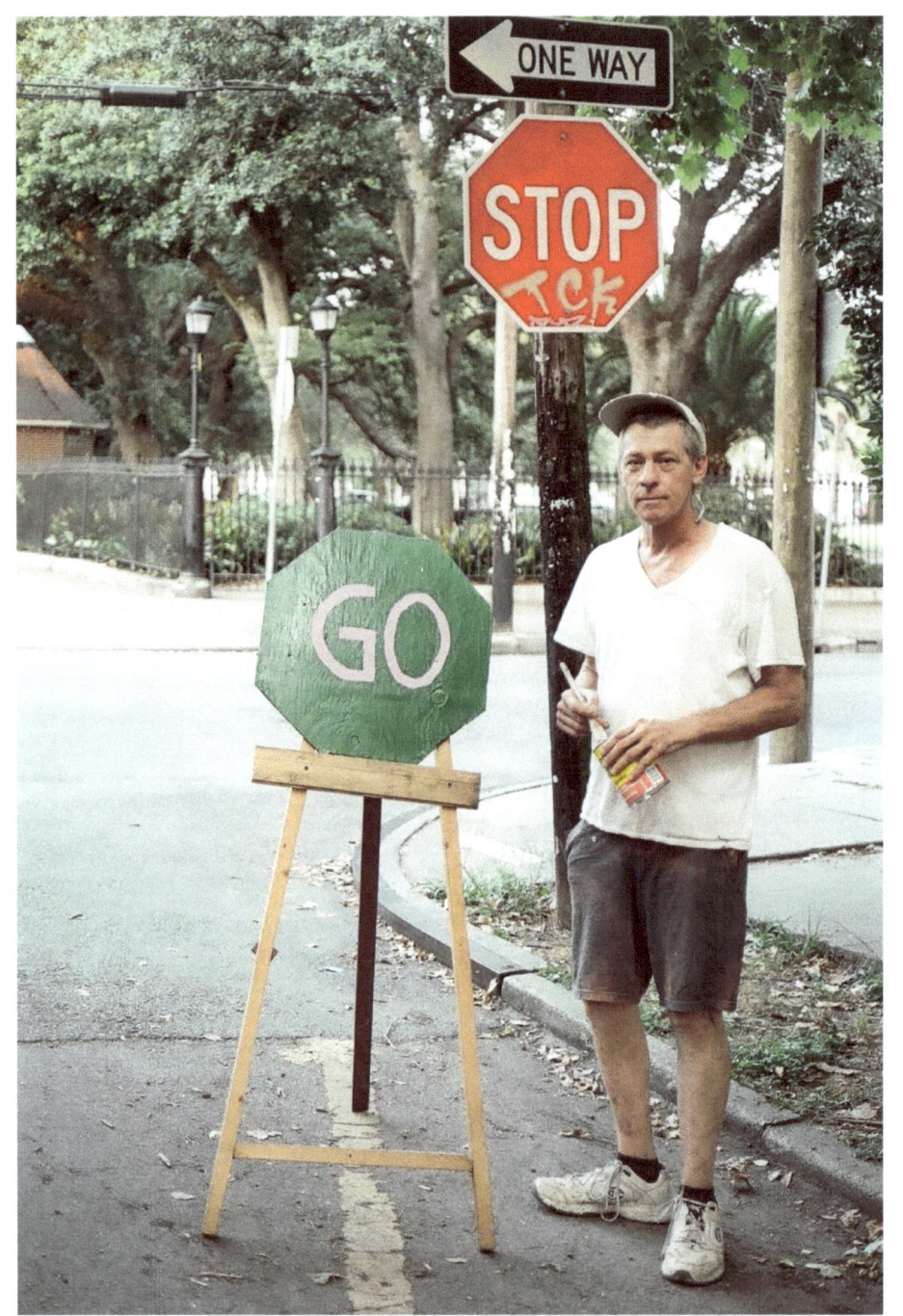

About the Artist